ISBN 0 85429 314 0

A FOULIS Motoring Book

This edition first published 1983

Published by:
Haynes Publishing Group
Sparkford, Yeovil, Somerset
BA22 7JJ, England

Distributed in North America by:
Haynes Publications Inc.
861 Lawrence Drive, Newbury Park,
California 91320 USA

Editor: Rod Grainger
Printed in England, by: J. H. Haynes &
Co. Ltd.

RALLY
NAVIGATION

Martin Holmes

Foreword

I was very pleased to be asked by Martin Holmes to write the foreword to this book as his original edition of *Rally Navigation* was one of the very first books I ever read on the subject. Many of the lessons that I learnt in those early formulative years have stayed with me throughout my career in the sport and Martin can rightly lay claim to having influenced the course of rallying's first World Championship Co-Driver.

During the relatively short time I have been involved in the sport the cars have changed dramatically and speeds inevitably have become faster, but the co-drivers role has remained constant. His job has without doubt become more demanding, however the basic principals that I learnt from *Rally Navigation*, some eight years ago, are just as relevant today.

Co-driving has given me an immense amount of enjoyment and challenge. I hope that this book will open the door to many others to share in this exciting experience of rallying from the 'wrong' side of the car.

David Richards
Bicester
December 1982

CONTENTS

*The author navigating for Russell
Brookes in a works Ford Escort RS.*

Introduction

Many years have passed since the first edition of *Rally Navigation* was published, years which have seen much change in rally sport. Just a few years ago a Lancia Stratos would turn heads wherever it appeared, now it is banned from international events because it is too out-of-date! Mechanical technology accelerates at a most impressive rate. Now turbo charging is normal, four-wheel-drive has been re-admitted making it difficult to win a World Championship rally without this type of transmission system. However, perhaps the most effective changes have come through tyre development.

Although much else has changed in the last decade the human factor has remained constant. Rallying remains a sport where essential human experience cannot be bought or developed by technicians, which is why so many older drivers win the big events. In 1982, for instance, the drivers, except one, who won World Championship rallies were in their late thirties or forties! The reason is the same as ever: it takes years of trial and error to strike a winning note and avoid the pitfalls of inexperience.

The role of the co-driver is the same as ever. Decisions made in the middle of the night when the unexpected happens continue to spell the difference between success and failure. Three of the seven co-drivers to win world rallies in 1982 were over 42 years old! Each of them has spent a lifetime making mental notes of unhappy moments when they needlessly threw away their chances and resolving never to make the same errors of judgement again.

The new emphasis on technology has given an opportunity to the young driver who is able to adjust his or her driving style more easily, but the co-driver still has to guide the driver along the road which will enable him or her to use that developing style to best effect. Maybe in the next decade we will see development in human programming to reduce the effect of psychological weakness and, perhaps, the continued development of rally organisational techniques to overcome the need for the constant double-checking we spoke of in the first edition of *Rally Navigation*. But, however much men in laboratories try to correct the deficiencies of human performance, they can only write their programmes in the light of previous circumstances. In rallying, things are not so straightforward. Every circumstance is different to the last one, and you as co-driver are the man facing the situation which the manual hasn't foreseen.

I suspect my own co-driving career has come to an end but my work constantly takes me to rallies in every continent in the world where I watch and talk with competitors in action. The French have a saying that captures rallying — and the co-driver's role — exactly: *"plus ca change, plus c'est la mem chose"*. So long as we have a sport which demands a second human inside the capsule we currently call a car, the competitive performance of the driver will always depend on the performance of that second inhabitant. We used to call him a navigator. Currently most people call him the co-driver. It doesn't matter what the title is it's how he or she operates which matters. . . . Good Luck!

Martin Holmes

Chapter 1
So you want to navigate?

Well, do you? One of the beauties of rallying is that there is a place for you whatever your pretentions and ambitions and however seriously you want to take your sport. One of the special beauties of navigating as opposed to driving is that you can have much of your sport at someone else's expense! There are very few basic essentials that a person needs in order to have fun out of rally navigating. I think a love of cars is the most basic requirement of all, followed by an enjoyment of travelling. In a lot of rallying a will-to-win is something you need to make your sport worthwhile, but even that is not essential if your rallying is centred around your motor club's 12-car practice runs, with your girlfriend for company. In quite a number of rallies a cast-iron stomach is a Good Thing, but the daylight special stage rallies are very easy on uncertain tummies, even if in turn they demand inordinate fearlessness on the part of the navigator, coupled with a blind faith in your driver's abilities.

Something more important than having full qualification in navigator ingredient is knowing what you want and what you enjoy, for in this way you can aim at the sort of rallying that gives

you the fun you want and you avoid the frustrations of doing something else. Knowing your limitations, knowing the sort of errors you might make, being on your guard for the sort of thing you may not be very good at, is part of the sport. If there is any one factor that is common to all successful rallying it is the ability to think ahead. Thinking ahead stops you doing the events you will not enjoy, stops you falling foul of organisers who are less adept at their job than you are at your navigating, stops you being caught unaware when the organisers try to spring surprise instructions on you, and stops you from taking the wrong things for granted. There are constant pressures on you as a navigator, at whatever level you compete, not to keep stock of what you do, or to make you so engrossed with the problems of the moment that you stop thinking ahead. Sometimes these are the intentions of the organisers. Sometimes these are the natural circumstances in a sport which caters for fickle cars and even more fickle drivers. In whatever way you are tested, the quicker you can recover your composure the better you will be rallying.

Another ingredient common to all sorts of navigating is a facility to allow your driver to be the boss, but at the same time make certain that he does things the way you want. This is psychology more than rallying, it must be the sort of thing women face every day in their lives, but at the risk of male navigators being considered 'old women' by their drivers it is something you must cultivate. It is a wonder there are not more successful women navigators in rallying. As a breed, drivers are extrovert and navigators are introvert. Drivers love to succeed and impress, navigators love to succeed only to satisfy themselves and their drivers.

How to find the right sort of rallies

A navigator without some basic map-sense is of little use, and if you do not enjoy the challenge of route plotting, of understanding contour lines and symbols, of scales and latest editions, you will be missing some of the groundwork upon which a future usefulness will depend. There is little to compare with the evening motor club run, even the treasure hunt, to develop this map-sense. You learn all manner of things about maps and map-reading on this sort of exercise that you will not have time to develop later on: things like the way you mark routes on your map, the way you interpret a map and give instructions to your driver. I took up navigating because I enjoyed maps as well as cars, and the combination spelled rallying.

The trouble with basic treasure hunting is that the organisation is often unauthorised, or at least not under the aegis of the Royal Automobile Club Motor Sports Association (RAC MSA) which means that the format will often be of a sort that many feel brings

Navigators seek to remain in command at all times! Frances Cobb (far right) arranges for mere men to right the car in which she and Tony Pond had just overturned.

"Press on regardless". Dai Roderick, Castrol '75 Rally.

ultimate harm to the sport — or at least to the serious side of the sport. But so far as a young navigator is concerned the lessons learned on these events stand him very well when money and circumstances permit him to become more adventurous. Success on this sort of event will also mark the young person concerned as a navigator worth knowing, so far as the drivers are concerned, and in turn this means you are able to go rallying at other people's expense that much earlier in your career!

You will see in the next chapter something of the structure of the sport, of the importance of individual motor clubs in particular. The idea of having to belong to a club in order to be eligible to compete is something that many young and impecunious people find to be all wrong, but in fact it really works well from a great number of aspects. In particular, a

young budding navigator will find it very much easier to meet people able to complement a desire to go rallying through a club than through private advertisement, and there is an element of protection in dealing with a person who is another member of your club. The club concerned may not ultimately be the one you will find is best able to help you in your sport, but it will give you a grounding. Members will talk about magazines and events, problems and people and they may organise events to which other clubs and their members are invited. A motor club will start you on your way, and give you an idea of the opportunities that lie ahead.

You will probably find that your rallying tastes will change over the years, certainly the more different types of rallying you have behind you the more use you are when you tackle something new. It is a source of constant amazement and disappointment to me that lessons learned in one side of rallying often fail to filter through to other sides. A few years

"One of the beauties of rallying is that there is a place for you whatever your pretensions and ambitions".

ago there was one unholy row at the end of a daylight stage event. This was unfortunate but in view of the inexperience of the organisers, was not entirely unexpected. But what amazed me was the way in which the competitors went about trying to protect their own interests. Drivers were trying to prove points which only navigators could fully understand, navigators were absent at the crucial times when queries should have been made, arguments which were completely irrelevant to the issues were being raised. I was the navigator they were trying to beat on that occasion and felt faintly amused at what was going on, but if I had been a driver on the other side and realised my navigator had failed to use methods of argument and protest which road rallying had shown to be successful I would have been looking for another navigator without delay. There is little substitute for experience in a driver:

there is virtually none with a navigator. The moral, try different types of rallying. Maybe, even, you will enjoy one which you never thought you would.

Road rallies come at many levels of seriousness, though the really serious events were diluted during the mid-seventies culminating in new regulations for the 'eighties, before public pressure threatened the other forms of rallying as well. Initially cars were made quieter and auxiliary lighting restricted whilst, finally, the format of road rallies was changed. At the highest restricted level, routes over the trickiest lanes in the country were given out in advance: a real test for navigators who have to concentrate for hours on end at their maps. Iron stomachs, incurable insomnia, convincing persuasion with marshals and organisers are all essentials here. Every year of experience helps in top-level road rallying, for there are always tricky junctions and funny little roads to know about, even though recent issue maps and proprietary 'marked maps' help a lot. The long distances

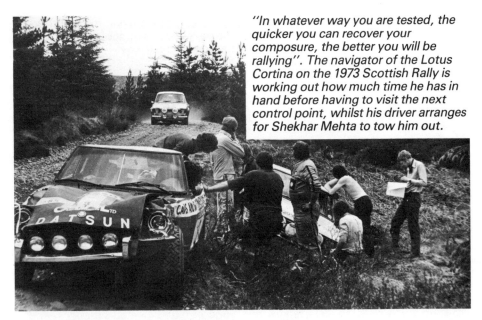

"In whatever way you are tested, the quicker you can recover your composure, the better you will be rallying". The navigator of the Lotus Cortina on the 1973 Scottish Rally is working out how much time he has in hand before having to visit the next control point, whilst his driver arranges for Shekhar Mehta to tow him out.

One of the biggest joys of rallying is the battle with a rival. There is little point in concealing information about your stage times. Here, Henry Liddon asks Bjorn Waldegard his times in the late stages of the 1973 RAC, which Liddon won (with the help of Timo Makinen).

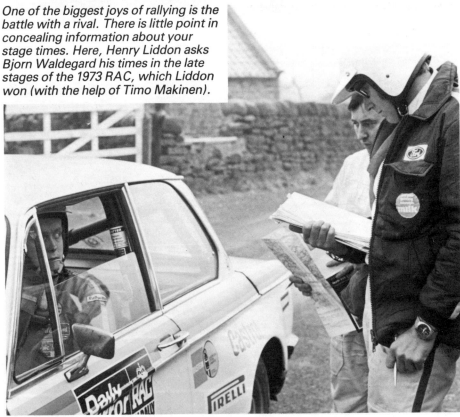

used as competitive sections demand a special psychology from navigators, who must keep their drivers hard at the sport when tiredness ebbs enthusiasm away. Road rallying offers almost incomparable experience in rallymanship, which is of inestimable help when you proceed to higher levels, but its very sophistication means that you have to concentrate at this sport to be successful and this in turn leads you away from interest and awareness in the other types of rallying. Navigators good at both road and stage rallies are very rare. One such person is Ian Grindrod, who has for many years navigated in *Motoring News* rallies and successfully moved on to partner Tony Pond and Jimmy McRae in the highest grade World Championship rallies.

It is amazing just how much there is to learn in road rallying. I started off with what I thought was an incurable car sickness problem but this was eventually almost entirely cured. I thought I would never stand the effort of travelling all afternoon to Wales, of

navigating all night and then returning the next day, but gradually it became natural. In those days there was little alternative sport other than staying locally to do area association events. Nowadays we have so many other events that I wonder if people will keep at road rallying when so many difficulties face them. I hope they will, for the sense of fulfilment in directing without error a driver around a really tough night rally is immense – or so I am told by those who claim to have done it!

Local association events, particularly in the South and East of England, tend to use less demanding territory and often incorporate more trickery in navigational instructions and, in closed-to-club events, it is even more so. These instructions mean that navigators have to be more able to cope with unexpected situations, and

Navigators should never be too proud when it comes to messy jobs, but it is nicer when someone else can do them for you.

Navigators form even more of a common factor in rallying than do drivers. They keep active in the sport for much longer than the average driver. Arne Hertz (left) and Hans Thorszelius represent two extremes. Hertz has won rallies with many different drivers whilst Thorszelius has usually only accompanied Waldegard.

this gives excellent training. You learn to keep cool and handle the instructions calmly. It is amazing just how much the tenseness of the occasion will sap your confidence. The instructions which these events give also increase your map-sense. They teach you to gauge distances, spot the quickest routes, find the entrances which the maps have almost hidden. The very ''trickery'' of these events means that you cannot take them seriously, for if you did you would soon find organisational errors which you could exploit and very soon the fun would go. People find that as soon as they start to want to win and become

disenchanted with these events it is time to move up the ladder.

At the bottom of the ladder we have treasure hunts which are social excursions. These are no places at all for the keen drivers but they are very good places for navigators who want a standing from which to progress and for anyone who wants to have his brain trained to work when travelling in cars. It is amazing just how many people have brains that just seize up at over 30 mph!

All road rallying depends upon competition on the public highway for calculation of results: anything indeed from thinly disguised road racing in the remotest corners of the country to touring the outskirts of urban areas looking for clues by the side of the road. Stage rallies are different, in that the rally depends upon competition on sections off the public highways, although on occasions penalties are given for lateness at certain control points, in order to keep the passage of rally cars under some control. Before there were as many special stage venues as we have nowadays, there used to be quite a few events which used a sprinkling of special stages within a road rally. These gave novelty and relief, but gradually more venues were available and it was felt that these combined events did not satisfy the demand for variety, for people wanted either one sort of rallying or the other. They did not want their sort of sport sullied by having to tackle the other. In some ways this was a pity as combined events gave followers of one side of the sport an insight into the opportunities of the other.

Stage sport has now become the major side, for there is no limit on commercial involvement as there is on road events. This means that people can afford to take stage sport seriously, which is encouraging for organisers. Organisers are able to aim at having their events included in any one of the increasing number of championships; this forces standards up and encourages other organisers in turn.

For many years we had a feeling among road rallyists — then the British establishment — that navigators on stage events were *sacks of potatoes*, and that a mechanic able to achieve an instant remedy for trouble on a stricken rally car — or indeed a lady friend who would otherwise lose interest in the man in her life — was a suitable choice for a rally companion of a driver. Then it started to dawn on people that navigators experienced in checking times and being persuasive with organisers were not without their uses. Finally we started to have a run of stage rallies which were lost by well known drivers who were deprived of success through timing troubles. Initial stubborn reaction was to blame bad organisers until it was realised that you gained success by overcoming other people's imperfections and using proper navigators. It is far better to win in the first place than have a good excuse afterwards for losing.

In the middle sixties we had only two major stage rallies in the calendar — the RAC and the Scottish Internationals. Then the Welsh came along with their International, the forestry authorities let smaller clubs have allocations, and slowly the movement started towards club stage events. The greater stresses on stage-rally cars means that there is more need for servicing of cars during an event. The stage-rally navigator (sometimes called a co-driver) becomes more of a tactician or strategist than a map-reader, in deciding how his service crews can best keep the rally car going.

Sometimes it is a matter of deciding which tyres to use and when to change them, sometimes it is deciding whether the crews can squeeze in one more service rendezvous point than originally anticipated, although on the majority of British events, servicing is strictly policed and restricted to certain nominated areas. All that map sense comes in handy! There is none of that poring over maps in moving cars that is part of road rallying, but there is plenty else to do. The forward-thinking bit stops you running out of petrol, saves your driver from being blinded as he rounds a sudden bend into sunlight, spots the dodgy arrow in the distance when the driver concentrates his eyes on the immediate hazards. I cannot list all the little things a navigator has to do during a stage-rally, for his job is to anticipate the unforeseen, to save his driver from having to worry about anything other than achieving the best times he can muster on the stages. Stage-rallying is less physical, certainly at club level, than road rallying but its mental demands are quite as great.

I hope I have not put you off navigating for good. Knowing your limitations is quite as important as having those elusive capabilities. There are quite a number of rent-a-ride navigators going the rounds these days: people with valuable commercial connections and hardly an ounce of rally intelligence or experience within them. Their drivers know this and take them along nonetheless simply because they would not otherwise be able to afford their rallying. The man who offers the whole range of navigator-assets does not exist; the most successful ones are those who make no pretence that they can do what they cannot. The things which keep you going in the sport are firstly good results — for these speak for themselves — and secondly personal reputation. And of course your personal feeling that next time you can do better, and wondering who you can persuade to drive you on the next event.

Chapter 2
How rallies are organised

In the first chapter you may have come to think that life for a navigator is one long battle between rallymen and organisers. It is! It is also very unfair that this should be, for rally organisers are almost entirely volunteers, and if we did not have these people we would have no sport at all. They are the salt of the earth. Rally organisers fall into two distinct categories, those who organise out of duty and those who organise in order to project their ideas of ideal sport. The latter category are usually active competitors themselves who lay on the sort of rally they themselves would dearly like to have entered, and almost without exception these events are the ones which are most enjoyable. Every chief organiser has dozens and often hundreds of helpers, and they are to me the people to whom we owe our sport. What keeps a person turning out weekend after weekend, very often right through the night, to enable other people to have their fun, is a mystery to me. An organiser at least has his authority as reward for his labours, but the organiser's marshals do not have this at all. They merely stand at their post and record what happens.

However good or bad an event,

there are many common rules to be obeyed. Some of these are statutory obligations, the breach of which can lead to prosecution, others are the common form of regulations which the RAC MSA, or the national sporting body concerned, lays down for every event which falls under its jurisdiction. In the first chapter we spoke of the importance of motor clubs. The RAC is the body approved by the Government for the control of motor sport in Great Britain and it delegates this approval through to clubs which are affiliated to it. It is possible for a non-affiliated club to organise events, but non-affiliated events are in practice the smallest events in rallying, although in many other forms of motor sport, non-affiliated clubs run events at the highest levels.

Rallies coming under the jurisdiction of the RAC MSA are graded into five levels: 1. Events in which competitors must come from the organising club alone ('closed-to-club'). 2. Where between two and six clubs can promote an event, but competitors must come from those clubs alone ('co-promoted'). 3. Events where one club invites a limited number of other clubs, or up to two area associations of clubs, to compete in its event ('restricted'). 4. Events in which anyone in the country can compete ('national'). 5. Events in which there is no limit ('international'). To speak as though there was no limit on who can compete is a little confusing, for along with this system of eligibility is a licensing system for competitors, and competitors can only compete in the higher grade rallies when they have had experience in the lower grades. The rules for the licensing of competitors often change but basically you need some form of licence if you are on an event of restricted or higher status. Details of these licences appear at the end of this book. Exceptions to the licensing system for competitors are extremely rare, but where circumstances demand, the rules can be relaxed. Licences are for two purposes: so that the RAC MSA as governing body can keep control of the sport, and to provide an indication that the competitor has adequate experience for a given level.

The RAC MSA acts in two ways to govern the sport: Firstly it acts in an agency capacity to the Department of the Environment by the statutory authorisation of rally routes; secondly it dictates the rules under which rallies are held. In this way, the RAC MSA sets an official seal of approval which other bodies, such as local authorites and police forces, can respect. This dual recognition of rallies — the statutory authorisation under the Route Authorisation Department as well as the authorisation under the RAC MSA rules — makes perhaps more demands on an organising body than the actual promotion of the event, which is itself a major task. Both stage and road rallies will probably need authorisation, in full or in part, and the basic rules under which RAC MSA recognised events are held are likewise the subject of common rules.

The RAC MSA dictates its own rules of competition in three forms: the General Competition Rules (which are about as forbidding as the rules of your motor club), Standing Supplementary Regulations which with the 'GCRs' are contained in a book currently produced annually by the RAC MSA and known as the *Blue Book* — in which the particular rules regarding the various types of motor sport are set out — and the Additional Supplementary Regulations, issued by organisers when plans for their event are announced, which you read before you submit your entry form for that event. These rules are complex, and are best followed by learning them backwards: by starting with the individual 'ASRs' (usually just referred to as 'regs') for the event which you have in mind to enter. There are many established navigators who achieved their successes without ever reading the 'GCRs', for these rules deal mainly with organisers' requirements, and their main relevance to a competitor is to show a competitor how a protest is to be handled.

It has often been said that you only need to know the rules in order to succeed in a bad rally, as organisers of good rallies make certain that they do not catch competitors out with obscure items in small print. Life is never simple, though, and not every rally is perfect. An indication of a good navigator is to see how often he wins bad rallies! I was very proud the day I had won my first restricted-status rally. It was a shock to read *Autosport* that Thursday and find their correspondent thought that the event had been a lottery!

What makes a good rally?

The best rally is one which the greatest number of people enjoy. To be a little cynical, one could say a good rally is the one you enjoy even though your great rival beats you! Good rallies do not just happen. Every one is the result of a lot of forward thinking — a typical navigator's exercise — and in fact most organisers of good rallies are themselves navigators rather than drivers. Good organisers think of the challenge they are planning from the viewpoint of the person who is competing. They spot the obvious shortcuts, the ambiguous instructions. They arrange the assessment of results so that the rally is won and lost upon the particular facets of the competition which they wanted. If you as a competitor have heard of the organiser it is probably because that person has experience as a competitor, and that event is likely to be enjoyable. It will also mean, almost invariably, that such an event will be over-subscribed, and unless your previous rallying record is enviable you will be lucky if you are able to compete. A lot of people enter only those events which they know will be really good, and often they frustrate themselves in having their entries returned. It is an understandable wish in any sport to pick and choose your activities, but in rallying this sort of thing often does not work, especially as more and more organisers allow entries to be filled up and only when all entries are to hand select those they allow to compete. It would be nice to have a first-come-first-served selection system, but sadly the postal system makes this unsatisfactory.

Planning which rallies to enter is an art in itself, but the structure of the sport makes things much simpler than they would otherwise be. A lot of clubs have their own championships; associations to which individuals' clubs belong, have championships; events which have national status or restricted events with national invitations often count towards national championships; and so forth. These championships offer much more than a prize for the best crews and even out the method by which standards are maintained. They offer a sort of club for people who have interests in a given sort of event, a chance of meeting fresh friends and colleagues of similar interests. Involvement in a championship will usually offer a greater likelihood of having an entry

accepted in the particular event you wish to enter, and consistent efforts in one championship will often help make your name better known − which helps when you think about tackling some fresh aspect of the sport.

Getting into the right club for the sort of rallying you wish to tackle is very much a hit-and-miss affair. Once upon a time the advertisements in *Motoring News* used to list all the clubs that were invited to the forthcoming events. This enabled the outsiders to see which clubs had the most invitations for 'their' sort of event. This practice has faded out, and the only way to find out the club of your choice is by systematically applying for all the regulations. The reports in *Motoring News* and *Autosport* magazines of events during the last year will often tell you which were the best − and the worst − events, and it is often a good idea to write to the organisers after a successful event asking to be put on the mailing list for the regulations of their next one.

How to enter

Entries for rallies are made directly to the club concerned (except in the case of events abroad, about which we will be talking later), by completing and returning an entry form and the relevant fee. Apart from the obvious matters of the preparation of the car and checking the particular requirements of each event, all events demand attention to three particular matters: the nomination of a club, the issue (where appropriate) of a competition licence and car insurance. To join most clubs you will need someone to propose and second your application, which if you are new to the sport will mean you will have to go along to a clubnight and find a couple of people for this purpose. To find out the secretary of the club you would like to join you will have to acquire a current copy of the *RAC British Motor Sports Yearbook* (the '*Blue Book*'), where the secretaries and competition secretaries of all the affiliated clubs are listed. The secretaries deal with club memberships (unless there is a special membership secretary as well), the competition secretaries deal among other things with invitations to rallies. As you can see, they make sure you are keen before you are able to take part! The rigmarole of joining clubs takes a little while: some clubs meet just once a month and have their committee meeting, when they consider applications to join, at some other monthly interval, so it can often be a couple of months before you have that coveted membership card in your hand. Not only do you have to be keen, you have to be patient as well. Getting your competition licence from the RAC MSA is a money-over-the-counter affair. Once these formalities are dealt with however, you have little worry about licences and memberships at least until the end of the year. The matter of vehicle insurance is a separate issue, however, and being the prime concern of the driver it is beyond the scope of this book.

Motor clubs are like most other clubs, the more you put into them the more you get out of them. It works in countless ways: you write little anecdotes about your rallying exploits in the club magazine and all of a sudden some other club members come up and ask if they can service for you on your next event. Clubs are obviously a means to an end — the 'end' being your rally sport — but it is surprising what other benefits they bring. The annual dinner and dance may retrieve a failing relationship with your girl friend; it is rare that rally folk go through their sport without making some important acquaintance within their club. Some clubs remind a member of the time when rallying was a jolly-good-show sport, and dirty hands were best left to chaps who worked in garages, and if you happen upon such a club be assured there are others more able to accept a serious competitor. Don't rush to join as many

as you can. If you are not happy with your club, wait until you have spoken to other people on the rallies that you enter and see which clubs find the greatest popularity. Incidentally, if when you first contact a club secretary you ask for a copy of their club magazine, you should have a good idea of what that club will be like to join.

It is only when you reach international competition that you no longer need the support of a club behind you. The RAC MSA takes the clubs network very seriously. It regards the official area association system as a stepping stone between it and the clubs themselves. It has quarterly meetings of association chairmen, when matters raised by clubs are discussed. This is the chief means by which club members can bring their views to the attention of the people who govern their sport. The main trouble with the club system is that whilst rallying is essentially an amateur sport an active competitor finds little time to concern himself with club matters and the people who act as mediators have few direct connections with the sport they seek to serve. The rules governing rallies in the UK are now generally the province of the Rallies Committee of the RAC MSA. Membership of this committee is by invitation of the RAC MSA's administrative committee and the Motor Sport Council. However, since a crisis in 1973 there are now far more active competitors and organizers on this committee. Their names appear in the 'Blue Book' and current committee members are willing to listen to constructive criticism of the rules.

It hardly seems possible or even important when you struggle to find a way of making your first entry that there are hidden ranks of officialdom in the sport. If they were not there, however, your sport would never have achieved its present degree of official acceptability. Most of the people concerned started off their rally sport in the not too distant past. It is one of the wonders of the sport that people often maintain an interest long after they retire from active participation. They are the ones who explain your sport to influential people. If we did not have such an elaborate structure it is hard to see how elders in the sport could play their part. Next time you are introduced to the aged Steward of the rally, call him 'Sir'. What he does in his spare time enables you to compete.

Chapter 3
Road rallying

The term 'Road Rallying' has only come about since the late sixties, since before then all British rallies, save for a few select International events, took place on the public roads. The idea of competing on closed sections on private land was very novel indeed, and not a little daunting for drivers whose cars did not have the benefit of the present knowledge on strengthening. In those days there was almost as deep a rift between the drivers' rallies, where routes were given out in advance, and the navigational events as there is today, between road and stage events. Today we still have that division in the style of road events, although official sources make little disguise of the wish to water down the 'drivers' events.

Road rallying is a three-fold exercise: driver, navigator and car. A successful event demands particular effort on the part of all three: if any one of the three is working less than well, the whole exercise is thwarted. The 'drivers' events are those that feature in the top league of road rallying. In these events there is no need for unnecessary elaboration of instruction, for the roads provide their own challenge. The time the route is known

in advance has been gradually whittled down. I once entered a rally run by Knowldale Car Club, for years the pacemakers of rallying in the North, where they announced the full route several days beforehand, and sent it out with the final instructions. When the route was plotted one could tell what sort of fun would lie ahead. It was terrific just thinking about the rally to come. It also exposed for all to see the blatant breach of the average speed rules set by the RAC and the experiment was not repeated. If such an experiment were repeated today, it would again be short lived, if only because nowadays every self-respecting competitor would reconnoitre the route and make his own pacenotes. Life for the local inhabitants would not be safe!

In years gone by, the elaboration of the Ordnance Survey map system was primitive, with innumerable roads barely charted, or not charted at all. If you ever have the chance of looking at maps of Ulster, you will see what OS maps in Britain were like in the early sixties. When *Motoring News*, under the prompting of their then Rallies Editor, Stuart Turner, started their national championship for road rallies,

Snow rallies are amazing fun for competitors but bring great problems for the organizers through having to change routes at short notice. Peter Clarke, group 1 Ford Escort RS.

even they were tests of route-finding rather than the road 'races' they became later. Local knowledge was vital to a good performance — the timing at control points was to the minute and results were measured often in hours of lateness. One *Express & Star* rally boasted that three-quarters of its route was over 'white' roads: roads which the Ordnance Survey thought existed but had not surveyed recently enough to remember whether or not they were tarmac or unsurfaced. The same roads nowadays are plotted with the same precision as the roads in the Home Counties, which simplifies the navigation.

Drivers' rallies should take place within the hours of darkness, not just darkness for the first competitor, but for every one. It is a matter of safety, and means that road events have to be confined to the winter months if any real length can be used. Even the major road rallies are only at the restricted level: both for historical as well as policy reasons. Historically, insurance companies frowned heavily on national rallies (one seemed to have just as big an accident on a restricted event, however) so leading rallies voluntarily down-graded themselves to keep up interest among clubmen. Policies came into the picture at the end of the sixties when the, then named RAC gradually dissuaded organisers of national events from using public roads competitively. Navigation on these events is by map reference in conjunction with the Ordnance Survey 1:50,000 scale Landranger series of maps. Just sufficient references are given to define the control points which competitors are to visit, and to define the route to be taken in between. By specifying the direction by which competitors must approach, and sometimes leave, a control point, it is possible to define the most complex route around the countryside.

Much of the magic of road rallying is following narrow little tracks (Phil Cooper and Tony Viles BL Mini 1275GT)...

Just sometimes the organisers slip and allow competitors to double back, thus missing a particularly tortuous portion of the route and save time on the route to the next control. Such games are excellent fun, but usually it took the mastery and confidence of someone like Keith Wood or John Brown to exploit them. Lesser mortals fear there will be locked gates barring the way, or the road peters out into an impassable track, thus nullifying the advantage and forcing them to back-track and then travel the slower route. When the ploy works it is tremendously demoralising for your rivals to find you have stolen such an advantage on them.

Not every mile of a rally route is competitive. Often stretches of main road or sections through villages are treated as liaison, or non-competitive, sections. The very first part of a rally from the start revue to the first time control is usually one of these leisurely sections. Penalties for driving quickly in a non-competitive section are high as under RAC MSA rules, it is illegal to beat the bogey. These non-competitive sections are included to save local inhabitants the anxiety of having cars rushing past their houses and to ensure sensible driving on main roads.

The advent of the selective section

Road rallying had a major upheaval in the mid-sixties when John Brown, surely the brains behind more rallying innovations than anyone else, returned from working in France and tried out an idea which was the rage the other side of the Channel, that of timing sections to the second. By the mid-sixties, the maps had improved and reduced route-finding problems to such an extent that rallies were being won by the bare minute rather than the hour. Whereas a few years back the odd error by a marshal was of little consequence it was then becoming a crucial factor. Furthermore, a lot of rallies were having to curtail the extent of their competitive sections, so that a minute was not accurate enough as a unit of time keeping. Sections timed to the second were called 'Selectives', a misnomer since on the Continent these were the sections which were designed to be achieved within the bogey time, not those in which competitors were designed to be penalised. Although many felt this was introducing too great a competitive element into driving on public roads, in fact these sections took much of the pressure off organisers who otherwise were having to string inordinately long sections together in order to penalise crews. Selectives, as we will see in the next chapter, gradually demanded quite a different approach on the part of navigators, even though the sections

over which they were held were in other respects ordinary road sections.

The selectives saved a lot of major rallies from producing unfair results, and indeed it soon became a very bold organiser who risked running a major rally without incorporating at least one such section, for tie-deciding purposes. Some rallies on the other hand, used nothing else. Selective sections have often been said to create an off-on style of rally, a change for the worse after a long, hard grind of former days, when driving through the night was punctuated solely by stopping at control points and the petrol halts. Those long hard grinds were luxuries of a bygone age, unfortunately, for they were great fun.

With the advent of new road rally regulations for the 'eighties, however, all competitive sections can be timed to the second. Combining these with non-competitive sections where lost time cannot be regained has seen road rallies almost revert to the old style 'sixties events, although they do now incorporate a stop-go format similar to

. . . or finding your way past farmyards in the middle of the night. Billy Coleman and the author (Group 4 Ford Escort RS, Polish Rally).

Barrie Williams was one of the foremost Mini drivers on road rallies in the mid-sixties. Here he is with Richard Harper on the 1964 Rally of the Vales. Earlier that year he had won the International Welsh Rally with John Griffiths.

special stage rallies. The new rules have brought about a new competitiveness to road rallies and the sport owes much to the work of Ted Cowell in bringing about this change.

The RAC MSA has long imposed a limit of 30 mph average speeds on road rallies, and this was given the sanction of law in the mid-sixties. Whilst the RAC MSA alone ruled serious rallying, organisers were given a blind eye to breaches of the average-speed rules, unless there had been trouble in other directions. The Filldyke Rally in early 1964 was the subject of an RAC investigation because, says the legend, the RAC could not understand how the long, straight roads in East Anglia could have produced the heavy penalties among competitors. It is said that the

organiser was asked to comment on a finding that a certain section was set at 60, rather than a 30 average, to which the luckless man said it was a matter of regret. Several crews had covered the section in the time allowed, and he should instead have set it at an average of 70! This was the spirit of rallying in those days, when leading competitors used Mini Coopers and Cortina GTs, but obviously things would be changing when Escorts, Sunbeams and Chevettes were introduced, and the power they produced gradually went up past 150 bhp towards 200. The major rallies were organised by mature men fully aware of their responsibilities, but the lesser events were not always so well managed. Road rallying had shot its bolt by the early seventies and inevitably a watering-down became necessary, with cars becoming quieter and generally more standard. Then it started to pick up again towards the end of the decade until a general 'slowing down' seemed necessary during the early 'eighties, again for the sport's own good.

'Plot and bash'

Goodness knows from where this expression emerged, and what it means is equally obscure. It is usually used to describe a halfway style of road rallying in which route instructions by map reference and direction, or more obtuse means such as 'herringbone' or 'tulip' diagrams, are given at short notice to navigators. In this way competing crews wait at various control points for the moment they are to leave, completely unaware of where they had to head, when suddenly the instructions are thrust into the car and they are bidden to set on their way. In the early sixties this was all the rage: it was as suitable for the middle of Wales as the middle of Hampshire. Until 1966 you could have sections of one minute long, and when you have to stop each half-mile, interpret another instruction and then start off again, there is little trouble with the 30 average rule. After 1966 sections had by law to be of at least four minutes length, and this method was less popular. In any case, the major rallies had long since discovered the joy in presenting a complete route to crews. 'Plot and Bash' is still a method used on navigational rallies where variety is wanted and is very popular in the south and east of England.

Navigational rallies

There is room for plenty of fun with maps, and it is inevitable that cars should be part of that fun. Navigational rallies have no place in serious sport but numerically there must be far more navigational events taking to the roads each year than serious ones. The methods of defining the routes you are to take depend for their complexity on the guile of the organiser concerned — and how much he wants you to get lost! There are countless ways a route can be defined, and any well planned navigational rally thinks of more. The style of these events has remained constant over many years, only the names and the cars have changed. Their purpose is either to provide some form of motor sport over roads which are uninteresting for a serious organiser, or alternatively to provide a sport for those unable or unwilling to progress further. For better or worse these events will still come under the heading of 'Rallies'!

One of the most popular alternative systems of defining a route is to use the Tulip card, in which successive road junctions are depicted by little symbols, on which the road by which you approach the junction is shown with a ball and the road by which you are to leave the junction by an arrow. All the home internationals and many of the all special stage rallies as well use this system of instruction together with notes of interim mileages between instructions because navigators can follow the instructions without recourse to maps. Navigational rallies use these instructions without a note of the interim mileages, sometimes without even placing the symbols in order. Certainly you need maps in order to interpret the instructions. Another form of diagrammatic instruction is even more confusing: the herringbone is a long line with 'bones' on either side indicating the roads which join the intended route. The only snag is that the intended route is probably extremely tortuous, but for the herringbone it is like a piece of string that has been pulled straight. Then again the herringbone may not be a straight line but a continuous circle, and maybe the organisers do not tell you at which point in the circle the first instruction can be found. Sometimes a map trace is given. Some Continental rallies specify their routes by means of a transparent overlay with the route marked so you can use this to see which way you will have to go. In navigational events the overlay is a luxury. Sometimes the trace is of only a portion of the route, sometimes it is in mirror image form!

Organisers of navigational rallies have great fun planning their route instructions. There are limitless opportunities with numbers of grid references, spot heights and even road numbers. There is no end to the opportunities open to an organiser who wishes to inflict geometry or dead-reckoning calculation on competitors. For the navigator who wishes to progress on to more serious things these events teach you to think in a moving car and give you an excuse to pore over maps. To do well on one of these events is encouraging for the ego for you need a smattering of intelligence above all else, but never should you get too worked up over them. You just cannot take them too seriously or you will destroy their fun for other people. I was once asked to check the route instructions of a treasure hunt in which one of the clues was as follows, 'to find where the Hush Puppy had been'. Anyone living in Surrey will know that the competitors should have gone to Silent Pool. What neither I nor the organisers imagined was that half the entry would drive off to Peaslake!

Timing penalties

One of the most worrying aspects of any rally is the timing. Intelligent men unused to rallying read the SSRs, refer to the relevant portions of the ASRs and stare away blankly none the wiser. Spectators on stage rallies may travel miles to watch Tony Pond in action only to find, when they reach their destination, that he went through ten minutes ago as he was allowed to run ahead of schedule! Drivers often arrive hopelessly out of order because of their delay allowances. Every year some leading crew throws away its chances of success on a major event because the navigator misunderstands the timing system — and major events try to keep the system simple! Imagine the chaos on the road events, where

road timing is the essence of the results. Its all very simple, really, but it takes a few times before you fully get the hang of things!

Penalties are usually graded into two levels on road events, whereby the primary level represents the number of control points correctly visited and, by way of tie-deciding, a secondary level represents the time penalties incurred. On a straightforward event, the leading crews will be expected to visit every control correctly, so that the order will be decided by the number of minutes, and often seconds, of lateness at the various controls. In this way a competitor who visits every control, however long it takes him, beats a competitor who misses a control, even without time penalty.

Cars are despatched around the rally route at minute intervals and marshals record the time at which they clock in at each control. At the start of every competitive section the cars leave the moment they can, to give as great a chance as possible of attaining the target time for the section. It is custom, where timing is to the minute, to allow a competitor up to fifty-nine seconds grace at the end of the section before penalty is incurred, in other words timing is to the previous whole minute. Usually one tight section will follow another without a break, so if a competitor arrives at the end of the first section half-way through his allowed minute's start, and so he is more likely to suffer a penalty at the end of the second tight section. The classic road events have had long strings of these sections so that only the winner achieves the target time at the controls, and every other crew incurs penalties. The runners-up incur just the isolated minute loss, the next best drop minute penalty fairly regularly, the tail-enders incur penalties at every control, sometimes more than one minute at a time. The Rally of the Plains, under Allan Jolley, eventually became a classic at this and more recently the *Cambrian News* Trophy Rally is a strong challenger.

Some rallies have made it a challenge in the past to complete the entire route without time loss. For such events the number of 'clean sheets' was usually limited to the winner alone. Whilst the challenge of other rallies was to finish within the lateness allowance. For these rallies it is an achievement to lose no more than a couple of minutes at each control! It only takes fifteen controls where a couple of minutes are dropped at each for a competitor to fall behind the scheduled time by a half-hour and thus incur a penalty for failing to visit that control. Times due at control points are personal to individual competitors. If car No 1 is due at Time Control 10 at 12.15, then car No 41 will be on time if he arrives at 12.55, but should car No 1 arrive at 12.55 he will be ten minutes beyond his allowed time. If he left Time Control 9 on schedule and arrives at Time Control 10 at 12.20, he will have incurred 5 minutes penalty. We will see in the next chapter some of the special things for which a navigator must be on his guard. This principle of timing holds good for most forms of rallying, even stage events where Time Controls are usually incorporated at the start, half-way and finish. They certainly apply to navigational events, for the only way these events differ is the severity of route and the method of defining which way to go.

Once a time penalty has been incurred it cannot be reclaimed by catching up on time, although it is usually better to make the time up again, so if you lose further time later on in the event you will not be quite so likely to fall beyond an overall allowed lateness and incur a penalty for missing a control. Should you arrive early it is usually possible to wait at a control point for the time you want to come up, so long as you do not block the way for other competitors who are less leisurely than you (or indeed for non-competitors) although on some navigational events you are instructed to arrive at a specified time and if you are even seen beforehand you are given a penalty for being early. There are usually limits on the amount by which time can be regained, so that unless there is special exemption you cannot make up more than 25% of the time allowed for the section concerned, unless the section is short. I have always thought this unfair, and remember on one of my first major Welsh events Tony Fisher and Brian Melia, previous national champions, fell foul of this rule, even though the section concerned was a petrol halt. In fact it is a neat way for organisers to force crews to run nearer overall allowed lateness than otherwise would be possible.

Keeping check on time

The method of keeping time has varied over the years, just as the general trends in road rallying have changed. Once upon a time, when the 30-average was not easily attained by the machinery then used, times of arrival in accordance with GMT at each point for a hypothetical car No 0 were announced in route instructions. Then it occurred to folk that this led to a lot of unnecessary trouble checking penalties and working out the winners, when it was possible for each car to carry a watch in a sealed container, each car's watch set back one minute in relation to the car in front, so that each competitor was due at each control at the same time. Then, just as navigators began to learn how to work demon tricks with these watches a different system, inaugurated on the Targa Rusticana Rally, came into being. Here, the marshals held the official clocks and these clocks were set back one against the other. If a section was four minutes long, the clock at the control at the end of the section was four minutes behind that at the preceding control. The first control clock was set so that our ghost car No 0 arrived at 12 o'clock, and would therefore be due at every control at 12.00. The Targa was always

They all used to enter road events in the old days! Tony Fall on the Rally of the Vales, a "Motoring News" Championship event in 1964.

the classic event for trying to keep only a handful of crews within range of completing a route, and this device with the clocks enabled the competitors and organisers alike easily to spot when cars fell beyond maximum lateness.

After a while this Targa system came in extremely handy in quite another way. The 30-average gradually became an embarrassment to organisers as maps improved and cars got faster. Some form of concealment of the actual average which a competitor was expected to maintain became important, and there was no easier way than with the Targa system of timing. A route card might well say a car had four minutes in which to tackle a section, but if the marshals' clocks showed you were a minute late because you had taken your four minutes, there was a perfect answer to the problem. In this instance your 30-average had become a 40-average. Furthermore the moment the clockwork in the watches wound down, or with digital clocks when they were zeroed, the evidence had gone and the organisers were beyond official censure.

Road rallying has given a considerable amount of pleasure in the past two decades: in many ways too much pleasure. In the environment and social aspect it has tested the patience of many inhabitants beyond reasonable endurance, and once-every-six-weeks use of the roads rule for road rallies introduced in the early 'seventies was no bad thing. In sporting terms road rallies have often provided too much of a good thing for many drivers, who have stayed in road rallying longer than was good for their careers. In the early sixties, as we have seen, road rallies were the only rallies, but their success delayed the impetus to get stage rallying off the ground.

Road rallying is a method of becoming introduced to our sort of motor sport without the involvement of necessarily buying specialist equipment — or even a fully developed competition car. It seems clear that serious road rallying will never be with us again as it used to be known, but even the RAC cannot deny the demand for road sport in less strenuous forms. It looks as if those who hanker after sport in cars at night will have the navigational events for some time to come. Drivers must remember that success at sport in cars at night depends to an inordinate degree on the quality of the person in the passenger seat — and that goes for rallying as well!

Chapter 4
Preparing for road rallies

The regulations for an event, that is the ASRs, are the basis upon which that event is run, and a full understanding of the regulations will be essential if you are to have a command of the event. The very first thing you must do when preparing as a navigator for a rally is to obtain a copy — before you even decide to compete, unless you *have* to enter that rally because it qualifies for the championship in which you are interested. You need to see the regulations before being able sensibly to convince a driver to enter. If the event is a good one, there is little time for you to stop and study the regulations, as good rallies are filled with applications for entry very quickly.

All events authorised by the RAC MSA should have regulations in a standard form, a system easy for its officials to check, and a system which tells potential competitors all they need to know, or so you would think! Their being in a standard form, save for the specific items of detail relevant only to the event in question, sometimes leads organisers to change certain important aspects later when they realise the effect of the regulations as originally published. Furthermore the problems

of route authorisation and planning sometimes mean that an event does not eventually turn out the way the organisers had promised in the regulations, and these changes are usually set out in 'Final Instructions' despatched to competitors a few days before the event. These 'Final Instructions' however cannot be used to alter the penalties laid down in the ASRs, a situation brought to the fore during the 1980 Calderford Trophy Rally and worth remembering by good navigators. Should there be changes which strike a fundamental change in the format of the event, a competitor will be told when the organisers acknowledge receipt of the entry. In the appendices to this book are shown the contents of the regulations for the Costi di Plenti Rally and the final instructions of the R.L. Brown Trophy Rally, both of which are fairly typical.

What do you look for in regulations? Assuming that you are considering a road event to enter, you can check easily that it will be a road event from the foreword, from the fact that the time of the start and finish and the dates show it is a night event, and by absence of any reference to stages. Also a road event will make much more

"Make certain things are where you would like them to be and you can find them without having to search". The inside of a Works Triumph TR7 V8.

reference to noise checks, damage penalties, and selective-section penalties and there will be different rules about penalties and rules for classification as a finisher. First thing to check is your eligibility, both by reference to club membership and licence holding. Then consider the form of the event, types of section, whether it has straightforward navigation or whether tricky navigational methods will be used (this tells you whether you are interested or not), and whether it is an event exclusively on tarmac roads or whether rough roads will be used (which is what your driver will want to know). A useful tip here is to study the list of acknowledgements, it will sometimes give away information about the route, such as petrol halts. Usually the contents of the regulations are evasive on these points, but the official foreword to the regulations will probably tell you. If you cannot tell from somewhere in the regulations

what to expect, then telephone the organisers and find out, but bear in mind if the organisers are either too shy or not thoughtful enough to put some clear description of their event in print, their vagueness will continue through the event and it will probably not be an event that you will enjoy. Your driver will probably wish to deal with the insurance aspect without delay, especially if he is using the organisers' insurance facilities, for a strict timetable has to be observed here. Elsewhere, where we look at the administration side of the sport, I will share some of my bitter experiences about making the actual entries, for this is an aspect that is common to all forms of rallying, and at all levels.

The next task for a navigator to deal with is assembling all the things he will need by way of equipment. I have a standard list which I keep in my rally bag, which saves the inevitable panic at the start if some essential is found to have been forgotten. My magical check-sheet is as follows:

Maps: those specified, with surrounding maps as well

Road atlas
Pencils, sharpener and rubber
Pills: sickness and headache
Money
Two Romers (one spare)
Magnifier, spare bulb and assortment
of plugs
Stopwatch
Crash helmet (only when regulations
demand — usually stage rallies only)
'RAC MSA British Motor Sports
Yearbook' (Blue Book) and 'FIA Year
Book' (Yellow Book): the latter for
international events only
Map-board for navigational rallies only
(preferably cardboard for safety)
Torch
Regulations and final instructions
Small change for telephones
Pacenotes, where applicable
Spare glasses and goggles
Overalls and jacket
Licences (competition and driving)
Club and championship cards
Intercom
Notepad
Calculator
    I also keep in my bag a
screwdriver, tape and pliers, in case I
have to fix the magnifier to the car
myself. I keep rally jackets, overalls
and walking boots ready for use. I have
often taken a railway timetable and
sometimes even an airline timetable,
and I usually take sweets with me, but
these are more luxury than essential
commodities. Sometimes there has
been some item which I know I am
missing when we leave for the rally,
but I have found this list perfect for
saving the unexpected panic. On
highly navigational events you need
equipment that is special to the task of
solving the problems, like tracing paper
for transcribing the map traces, and
sometimes on really mathematical
treasure hunts rulers, compasses,
protractors and so forth. The use of
this equipment is beyond the scope of
this book. I have also often taken an
electronic calculator with me, and
found it essential on international

*"Only a week away and still no engine
in sight". Tony Fowkes' Ford Escort
RS 1600 just before the 1973 RAC
Rally, on which he and Bryan Harris
came 9th overall.*

events where the rallycar tripmaster is wildly inaccurate, and at the end of rallies where penalties are calculated in terms of points, which need hasty checking.

A book could be written about maps alone. They are perhaps the centre of everything navigational. The regulations tell you which maps the organisers expect you to need, and in road rallying they will tell you which edition as well. Unless the organisers particularly say you must use an older edition, I always use the latest edition there is. With every edition the main road improvements are marked, even if the little minor roads which have lately been built or changed, are not. A corner cut on a main road throws even the expert navigators out. Having adjoining maps is a precaution for the rare occasion where an organiser is minded to take you away from the specified maps by way of instructions which are thought to be sufficient for your use, but insufficient for you to know where you are should a

It is not just accidents which make belts essential. They hold you firm and make you less susceptible to cornering forces. Also they stop you having to grimace like this poor fellow if your car suddenly encounters a bump. "Keep your belts done up tight".

breakdown occur. Sometimes an organiser might issue a map with control points marked, but without any guidance as to which roads you can safely take. This is no trouble if that map is a duplicate of one that is specified, for here you can refer to the markings on your personal copy. It is when he issues you with a copy of an adjoining map that your confusion will be saved only if you have your own copies of that adjoining map. Sometimes, very rarely, it is quicker to choose a route between two consecutive controls by a route on an adjoining map. Having a collection of adjoining maps is an expensive luxury, but just sometimes it pays handsomely. Peter Bryant (who by strange coincidence used to be a map stockist!) used an adjoining map to gain a minute's advantage down in Somerset on the 1972 Rallye Bristowe. He was lucky in that it was on an early section, the route was issued some hours in advance, and it was possible for the route to be checked to see whether the alternative was quicker or not. With a maximum of two hours allowed for plotting these days, it is still possible to mimick Bryant's initiative.

Marked maps are those on which personal notes have been added. The sadistic might refresh their memory of a route by adding notes such as 'RIP, Joe Bloggs' Escort Twin Cam', though it would be smarter and less cumbersome for a bend that is nastier than a map would suggest to be indicated by a ring and an '!'. Which roads are passable and which are not is the usual marking. Assuming that every coloured road on OS maps is passable, it is a good plan to mark the passable white roads in a distinctive colour so that they stand out and are more easily followed when the rally car is in motion. Back in the time when Stuart Turner wrote his original definition of Rallying (the early sixties) it was a good plan to mark with a hefty 'X' a road that was not passable, but since those days a lot of 'X' roads have become passable, and often a road impassable in bad conditions becomes usable in the dry. Another old fashioned marking was the way that gates opened; which side of the road you would find the hinges and which way the gate opened. Nowadays all public gated roads must have the gates left opened and marshalled during a rally, but if the rally is undermanned, an unattended gate may get closed on purpose by an enterprising crew or spectators as happened in the 1979 Cilwendeg Rally. It is wise to know about roads with gates which are usually locked, so that you will not be tempted to take that road unless the instructions make it clear that the road is to be used.

The two other main features to be noted on maps are unmarked hazards and misleading road junctions. It is frightening that the very features you would want to know about when you are rallying, the downhill hairpin or the sudden, narrow, S-bend, may not appear on the map. Remember that OS maps were not originally designed for rally navigators! Once you meet such an obstacle mark it on your map for future reference. There is usually good reason behind map errors; it could be that the errors occur in areas where surveys are rarely carried out, it is often that there are physical limitations as to the degree of details that can be shown. One can often judge in advance the circumstances in which maps might be wrong. Just sometimes, as in the maze of lanes north-east of Dolgellau, the maps adjust themselves to the complexity of the area. In this case there is a lane that is shown much narrower than other yellow roads. Even so there is a bend in that region that is not shown. One trouble with OS maps is that an average road, as portrayed on a map, is some 60 yards wide. Anything that happens within an area of 60 yards of a road is going to be inaccurate or not shown at all. When the ASRs specify several adjoining maps (and when funds permit) it is useful to cut a strip four or five kilometre squares deep from an old map and stick it onto the border around the adjoining map. If there are several map changes in quick succession you will be glad you did it!

The motoring magazines carry advertisements for people who offer marked maps of the popular rallying regions for sale. They all carry the difficulty of personal interpretation of their markings, but at least they give some warning of trouble for a navigator who has not rallied extensively on the map concerned. This special marking is something of the icing on the cake. If you will be expected to plot your map references at short notice, it is wise to mark on the maps you know you will use the grid numbers right across the middle of the

Even though proprietary map magnifiers are available like this from Don Barrow Products, most navigators regard their magnifiers as personal. Some people modify magnifiers they buy, like cutting holes in the side so they can mark maps with pencils whilst illuminating them at the same time. This magnifier is unmodified.

map. Much time is lost by scanning your eye across or up the map to the numbers which appear at the margin, and often errors in plotting happen when the eye jumps a line. Sometimes you find that there is another road in the adjacent kilometre square, and you wonder why a control is not manned when you reach it! A rallyist tired of maps is tired of navigating. The new, paper covered, second edition Landranger maps already have these extra grid numbers overprinted — a useful legacy gained from the military O.S. maps. Until now, these overprinted military 1:50,000 maps have been a much sought after commodity on rallying's 'black market'. The inclusion of a road atlas is to enable you to make your way home from outlandish places where you personally end your rally as well as helping you with scheduled journeys to and from events.

Pencils are the tool of the navigator's trade. Even if you never made an error in plotting and you never needed that particular map again, the organisers are always capable of changing the route after it has been plotted, and leaving you to erase what you have already plotted. Fibre tip pens are popular for colouring in the roads which you reckon are passable — for careful colouring can neatly fill in the parallel lines which form the white road on the map. Some people prefer a felt tip pen, so that the borders of the road can be visibly overrun, in case you mistake a road you have coloured in for one that the map makers have. There is no great advantage in using very soft pencils, for although such pencils leave a heavy line that is easily seen at night, they leave smears over the map when it comes to rubbing them out, ready for

Map magnifiers are useful for general illumination. Here Barry Cooper uses his magnifier to throw light on a time card. This saves the delay in the marshal taking the card out of the car. Note also he has the card on a small board, which enables the marshal to write on the card firmly, and again saves the delay of the marshal finding some other firm surface.

the next event. I use HB pencils as a good compromise, although by far the most popular is 2B. Incidentally I leave routes on maps as long as I can before rubbing them out, as they act as a good reminder about problems on that map for the next event. If you drop things on the floor of a rally car they usually remain on the floor until after a rally, so take enough pencils to last. Special seat brackets, fire extinguishers on the floor, maybe even layers of mud on the floor all help to conceal small items that have been dropped.

There has been much dispute about anti-sleep pills, and apart from the laws about driving under the influence of drugs (against RAC MSA rules as well), they have seldom been found to be of any use. One can continue, with a little practice, for a considerable time by having cat-naps, by conserving energy, by being reasonably fit and by planning one's meals, but the best anti-sleep pill of all is simply concentration, so keep the concentration going even in non-competitive sections. Sickness pills are another matter. Generally they fall into two categories: those producing a side effect of drowsiness and those making you dry in the mouth. It is obvious which sort is the better for night rallying! Sickness has been my problem for years, and even now I find that I am susceptible if I have had a bad head cold, or if I fail to take the pills the proper time in advance. Headache pills are another wise precaution to keep you going, though it is amazing how much the excitement of the moment takes your mind off toothache, flu or a bad cold.

Money is another topic we will discuss in a later chapter, but however much you plead poverty when making your initial arrangements with a driver, always take enough money to get you home from the farthest point in the route. Maybe, just possibly, you have a breakdown that is your fault. It's not nice to have to apologise and then to have to ask for your fare home. Sometimes it's best just to disappear off into the night.

Romers and magnifiers are two of the navigator's most treasured possessions. Romers are many and varied; find one you like and stick to it. Added to this, whenever you tried to plot a reference with other types of romer you seldom came to quite the same result! Try to get one with points of the compass marked on, or write them in yourself, in the heat of the moment it is amazing how a NE approach can be plotted as NW. Homemade romers have never worked properly, for ready-made ones are surprisingly precise and their low cost makes a hand-made one uneconomical. Homemade magnifiers on the other hand, are quite the rage for everyone wants a magnifier to suit his own requirement. Some want them extra-lightweight, some want them bendable, some want rheostats so that the light can be dimmed, some want romers etched into a transparent base, some want simple scales likewise inset into a base. Some want a hole cut into the side so they can place a pencil mark on the map whilst looking at the map through the magnifier, some are just plain frightened at the cost of a ready-made one. About the only two features that every magnifier has in common are a lens and a lamp working off the car battery. Little handy magnifiers can sometimes double-up as a hand-held inspection light, certainly any that have reasonably bright lights and have no light-diffusing base can be used as a lamp for looking around inside the car. I have usually used a homemade one for the sake of expense, without a base.

Stopwatches are of little use on ordinary road rallies, as timing on these events is based on what the official watch held by the marshal says. A wrist chronometer is essential for stage

rallies if the expense can be spared, for it will save a stopwatch from swinging around the neck and tangling with the romer which is usually also kept on a length of string. Stopwatches are fun things to have to check by how much you have beaten the man behind you on a given section − if you can wait long enough to find out. With the advent of electronic clocks we can have backwards-reading stopwatches which you can set to read some time in the future, and which you can read at a glance to see how much longer you can spend at a service point, halfway cafe and so on. At this point you should be materially complete, and all you now need is to be factually complete. Some things you need to know can be found from the regulations or final instructions, some things can only be gleaned by careful ferreting from people who might be concerned. From the regulations you will need to have the following things clearly in your mind:

1: Control procedure. Be clear in your mind whether you will be given individual timecards or whether you will have to produce a timecard sheet. Sometimes the procedure differs between time and passage controls. If you will have to produce a document to the marshal, make sure you have it readily available! Many navigators attach timecards to a clipboard to save them becoming mislaid, and to enable the marshal to have something firm on to which he can rest the documents he has to sign. If you will be given individual timecards, have somewhere save for them to be stowed, preferably in an envelope until they have to be surrendered to the organisers. If you mislay a card an organiser is at liberty to assume you never went to the control concerned, and often the regulations will warn you to this effect.
2: Is the timing to GMT or set Targa-wise? This is especially vital if you are running at the head of the rally, for you can clock in at controls late if you assume wrongly that GMT timing is being used. What is more; the

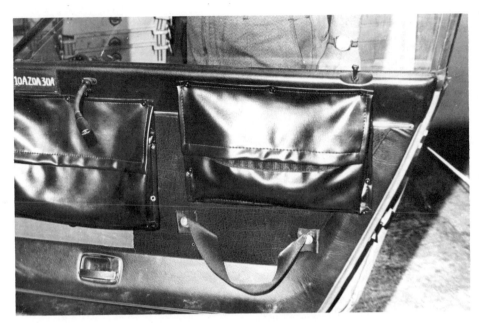

"Some friendly drivers attach a special pocket for your papers". The 1973 Datsun team cars were lavish in this respect.

competitors behind you might be angry if you lure them as well into lateness in this way.

3: Qualifications for finishing? Like the two items above, this will be clearly stated in the regulations, but similarly make certain you know the answer without having to check. Checking takes time, and you may well have forgotten where you put the regulations!

4: How late are you allowed to be at each control? Sometimes the last control of the rally is extended to 45 minutes permitted lateness before collecting a fail.

5: Are passage checks penalised at the same rate as time or time controls, or at a lesser rate? Often you can skip a passage check (which is just like a time control, save that the marshal does not take your time: in navigational events, you are sometimes asked to note some item of information at a passage check instead) at the loss of five or ten minutes' penalty. This does not help

you if your car is running well, as you would not normally expect to lose that five or ten minutes' penalty if you complete the route. It does help if you suffer trouble, or are running late and wish to stop yourself running close to your maximum allowed lateness.

6: What is expected of your driver in a non-competitive section? Rules do vary from the basic requirement of not making up time. Sometimes you must crawl along past a certain house or drive on dipped headlights instead of just extinguishing auxiliary lights. Your driver won't thank you if you are excluded for an infringement if you could have warned him in advance!

7: What are the rules for making up time in rest halts? Sometimes you make up how much time you like and other times you may be required to absorb all your lateness and re-start on your due time — if you're late you will lose more penalties.

8: Check whether you can catch time up fully on easy sections or whether you are limited to the '¾ rule', set out in the RAC MSA *Blue Book*. The new rules introduced in 1980 only allow time to be made up in competitive sections and between controls that are

"Sit in your seat and make certain things are where you want them to be. The simpler the interior, the better". This Terratrip instrument is as much as co-drivers need!

off the highway, *ie*, rest halts. It is becoming popular practise to designate petrol halts as rest halts, but not always, so beware.

These eight points are vital for a navigator to have in his mind. There are other things that are worth knowing in advance, which the regulations will not tell you about and which you might find out by asking an organiser direct. The most important is knowing how many miles of loose surfaces you can expect on the route, to enable your driver to make the correct choice of tyres. It is far better to come properly equipped than have to wait till you have plotted the route, and have to make a change minutes before the start. It may well be that you could even then make an error, by assuming that an unknown stretch of ten miles of white road means that

there are ten miles of rough roads. There is an increasing habit of the Ordnance Survey to mark the whole of tarmac dead-end roads as white — even if a little track enables you to regain another tarmac road at the other end. It may even be that the road has only recently had tarmac.

It is often fun to know in advance if a route will use some famous stretch of road, so you can make your own pacenotes of that stretch and have some idea of how professional rally drivers live. Only long stretches of roads without junctions are any use for this purpose, as these roads seldom pass many houses, so your looking at such stretches will not cause disturbance. Never do anything to draw attention to yourself, for if you do that road might suddenly be blacked to future organisers. Never, for this purpose, look at roads driving your rally car. Even if you do not go to look at a road beforehand, there are few pleasures quite like the pleasure of anticipation, and rally drivers enjoy this pleasure in good measure. Organisers who are secretive about their events for no reason are often denying competitors much of the joy of competition. Sadly inconsiderate actions by competitors on previous events give them good reason!

Most of the preparation for your rally is now done. If you have done your homework carefully you will probably have the odd query. It is usually best to telephone an organiser with a query before the night, for on the night the man best able to answer the query will be rushing around doing essential jobs. Further, it could be that you have spotted a point that the organising club never thought about. Try to have a look at your rally car before the night, even if it is depressingly short of an engine, axle or lights! Sit in your seat and make certain things are where you would like them to be. Make certain the flexilight — the lamp for general map illumination on a flexible stalk — is not too floppy, and if it is make certain that it is restrained in some way. Make sure you know where things are, especially the equipment necessary to change a wheel. Nobody ever seems to do it at club level, but just a single practice run at changing a tyre can save a minute should you have to do it in earnest. Make sure your jack is wound down so it will fit under the car with a flat tyre. Also, make certain that there is a firm base to the jack so it will not sink into the ground if you have to change a tyre on an unsurfaced road.

Check your safety belts, so that they are properly adjusted. Some cars have belts that are incredibly difficult to adjust, so it is best to do this before you set out rather than in a wet car park in the dark at the start of the rally

itself. Check that your magnifier fits the plug socket in the car — and has sufficient length of flex, and make certain where you will keep your papers. Standard cars usually have glove pockets — though sometimes the lids fly open and scatter the contents all over the car. Some friendly drivers attach a special pocket for your papers — and especially the time cards. If you have nowhere else to put things, you might be able to stuff the time cards inside your shirt, though it does not endear you to the officials when you hand them a series of screwed up, sweaty cards. Nor does it do much good if your shirt becomes untucked in the bucking you will have, and your cards are scattered to the winds the moment you step out of the car.

A good previous night's sleep is all that a reasonably fit person needs to stay awake on a night event though practice certainly helps. Try to avoid travelling down to the start of the rally with your driver unless economic circumstances dictate otherwise. You do not want to be concerned with your driver's flaps and panics, you certainly do not want to be stopped from getting to the start early because of some trifling trouble with the car. The later your driver is likely to arrive at a start, the more important it is for you to be there already and make the organisers reserve your entry ready for the moment when his car swings into the scrutineering bay. The only trouble is that the waiting is terribly bad for ulcers, and standing at a start when all the others drive off into the night and you have no driver is as miserable as sitting in the bath when all the water has flowed away.

Chapter 5
Road rally techniques

In all the years that I have been involved in club and national rallying, nothing has dulled the sense of excitement at the start of an event. It does not matter if it is a club twelve-car event or a national championship round. Cars start arriving in the town where the start takes place, hours beforehand. Some come on trailers and seek anxiously a place they can unload and leave their equipment safely overnight — and where they will be able to retrieve it next morning! Some drive their competition cars and tour the town a half-dozen times looking for somewhere to eat — a place that is both open and that is fit for their pocket. Slowly more and more people arrive as tea-time draws near for the local inhabitants and the first slight chill of evening sweeps through. Somehow people become caught up in the tension of the occasion. Instead of hastening about their business they stop and stare at the invaders. An evening when a rally starts in a town is an occasion. Even when there is not a single notice telling outsiders where and when the start will be, word gets around and people make their way at the appointed hour to see the action. A rally creates magic in the air, and it is

this very same magic that will destroy your carefully conceived plans and lure you into making mistakes or forget things that you never thought possible.

From the moment you arrive at the start, you are in charge of your operations. It is up to you to ensure that whatever should be discovered is discovered. It is nice when your driver notices something which helps you in your work, but for him this is a time to relax and worry about nothing more difficult than satisfying the scrutineers that your car is rally-worthy, filling up with petrol and cleaning the windscreen. Even these things should be done under your supervision, in case he says the wrong thing to the scrutineer or tops the petrol tank to the brim when there is another petrol halt after 50 miles! He is going to need his energy through the night. A moment's lapse from him can spell a bent wheel or worse.

The main jobs at the start are scrutineering, noise check, signing-on and route plotting. Scrutineering is a thankless task and is never performed systematically. Regulations often list things that will be given particular attention, but all of a sudden there may be an unwanted purge on advertising

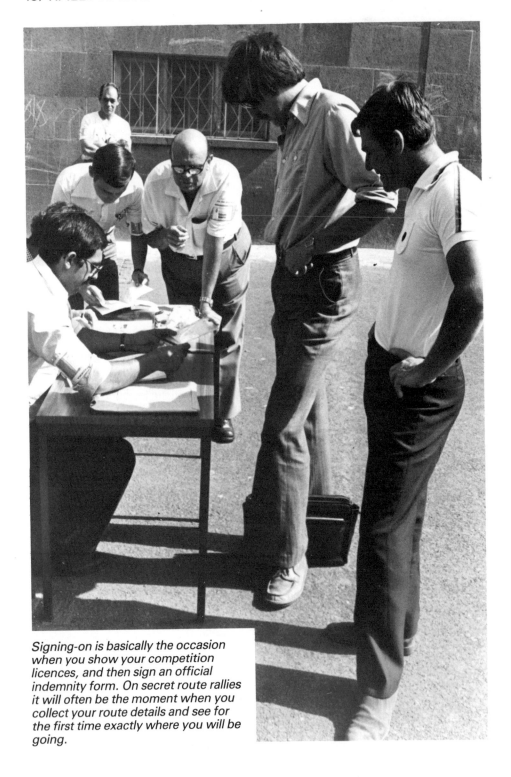

Signing-on is basically the occasion when you show your competition licences, and then sign an official indemnity form. On secret route rallies it will often be the moment when you collect your route details and see for the first time exactly where you will be going.

Even scrutineering should be done under your supervision, in case your driver says the wrong thing!

on the cars or some detail like the fixing of the seats to the floor. Scrutineers are all volunteers, so civility to them, even in the face of infuriating odds, is essential. I have almost never met a scrutineer that has not conceded some compromise in a difficult situation, and where a compromise is likely to be required, it is your job as navigator and 'brains of the team' to dream one up. Noise checking too can bring its problems. Noise meters vary from event to event as do the sites of the test. If your car fails at first, it is your job to check that the test is being carried out correctly — even a nearby wall can affect noise readings. One notorious noise judge always used to make everyone nearby stand perfectly still during the actual meter reading, ''it affects the magnets'' was his reason — now, that excuse is

A scrutineer examines various features of Russell Brookes' Group 1 car. In the ordinary way the only things a navigator must do at scrutineering is to have any important pieces of paper at the ready, but be prepared for a battle of wits in case you have come to some compromise solution on a tricky point. 1974 Burmah Rally.

always worth a try! Signing-on is the formality of producing your licence (or paying a forfeit if you have left it at home) and signing an indemnity. You will probably pick up all the paperwork

that is needed although you will have to wait for your route card, usually given out two hours before your start time in exchange for some form of card. Always make sure you know what you need to collect your route, and *always* arrive at the hand out point early.

Plotting the route is the first obvious job you have to perform. Always choose the best-lit place you can find, for the dimness of the interior light in a car is ideal for missing the little marking on the map which represents the correct route. A number of cars fit a strip light that floods the car with brightness, but if you are not so lucky as to have this, see if the start garage has a corner of a showroom into which you can nestle into with your maps. Failing all else, try mounting a small reversing or side lamp to a piece of wood which can be jammed behind the roll cage and plugged into a dashboard socket — but remember to stow it away safely afterwards. The easier it is for you to plot, the quicker the plotting will be done, and the sooner you will be able to check on the final preparations for the rally — and be able to check your route with a friend. Remember though, if you have spotted a short cut not to mark it on your map until you've checked the routes! To see the leading navigators before an important road rally would make you think some religious rites were being performed. One navigator will dash into the driver's seat of a rival car, and then return to his own seat for another navigator to rush into his driver's seat. Speed down the lanes and accuracy of finding your way are quite different challenges without the added uncertainty of knowing if you had marked the route properly on your maps. I believe I still owe Peter Valentine for discovering two more mistakes on my maps than I discovered on his, from back in the 1972 season!

There is no hard-and-fast rule on how the maps should be marked. I have added to this book pictures which

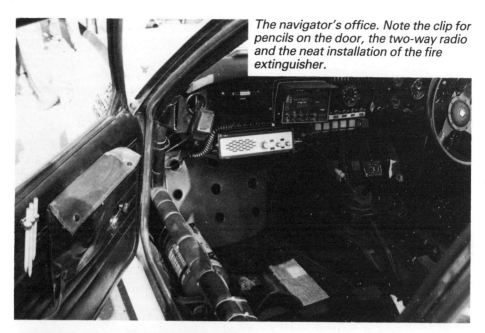

The navigator's office. Note the clip for pencils on the door, the two-way radio and the neat installation of the fire extinguisher.

"It can't be the right road".

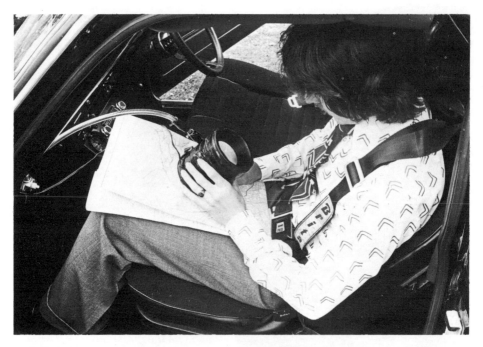

Reading the road. Note the way the map is folded to the area required, and as the navigator is not having to write on the map, no map board is necessary. Also that the lapstrap should always be particularly tight.

show that I mark competitive sections with a solid continuous pencil mark to the left of the road to be taken, with broken lines marking non-competitive sections. I like to show different types of controls in different ways — to save reaching for the time card for a passage check when maybe we will be handed a card at such a point instead. Not every navigator uses the one-continuous-line method, some even mark both sides of the route, others instead always mark the outside of any junction at which a turn has to be made. Marking a map is a personal thing. Whatever will enable you to stay on the correct route must be good. Some navigators like friends or drivers to read out the route instructions, which can work well, though I would rather be responsible for my own mistakes, and in any case reading the

instructions as the route is being plotted gives a navigator the maximum 'feel' about an event.

When the route which is known wholly in advance has been plotted, there is no need for any illumination in the car save for the magnifier, but on navigational events where the time for plotting the instructions comes within the time given for travelling to the next control, there are a few things you can do in readiness for the 'off'. Ensure that your map is folded so that the start is in the centre and that it is firmly held on a map board, which will enable you to write on the map without puncturing it with your pencil. It pays to study the area, to see the alternative routes you might take. It also pays to note the map reference of the start in case you are given a series of references or controls to visit in any order, so you can start your plotting with the nearest point. Sometimes on a navigational event you are already in possession of a road book which tells you the times or distances between control points. If this is the case, you can have fun in putting yourself in the position of the organiser and working out where *you* would site the first few controls, if you were in his place. On navigational events, the route will usually take the least obvious course.

As the moment draws near for the 'off', your driver will be beckoned by one of the start marshals to manoeuvre the car into line, and the sooner you dismiss the impure thoughts of life and concentrate on what you are about to do the better. This is not always easy. Sitting in a low slung car amid a crowd of young ladies leads to particular distraction! There is never any great rush, so if the start is off the highway, wait until you can see the road is clear before proceeding down to the first control. Always navigate your way to the first control, even if it is along main roads, getting the feel of distances in relation to speeds, this will help during the early sections. It is important to ensure that you keep your station in relation to both the cars ahead and behind, for there may be little room at the first control for shuffling the order of cars.

From the moment you leave the first control, your second and third obvious chores begin — that of reading the road to your driver, and of timekeeping. It is always worth asking to see the official's watch, not in this instance to check that he is reading it right, for if he isn't he has read it wrong for everyone else in front, but more to see that what the watch says coincides with what is written on your road book or time card, and to see if it coincides with your wrist watch. Our illustration of the route used on the Cilwendeg Rally provides a nice example of what rallying in difficult territory offers. When 'reading' the road in tight country, most drivers like distances

Route instructions on the 1973 Cilwendeg referred to in the text. Note that "Care at 'A' road junction" will now read: "Stop at Give Way", which will be an official check point.

Time 3	...	...	327½	454	NNE	SSE	10.48
Time 4	...	...	311½	440½	ENE	NNW	10.52
Time 5	...	...	319¾	470½	SW	E	10.59
Passage 2	...	...	340½	476	SW	NW	
Time 6	...	...	329	497	SW	NNW	11.07
Time 7	...	...	365½	468½	NNW	SW	11.15
TAKE CARE AT "A" ROAD JUNCTION at 378½/463							
Time 8	...	...	407½	447	NW	SE	11.22
Neutral Section to Time 9							
Quiet Zone at PRENGWYN							
CARE AT "A" ROAD JUNCTION							
Time 9	...	...	420½	428	NNE	SSW	11.32
Time 10	...	...	438½	418	SE	ENE	11.40
Passage 3	...	...	461	395	ENE	WSW	
Time 11	...	...	449½	370	NNE	SSW	11.55
RELAXED SECTION from Time 11 to Selective 1 Start							
Selective 1 Start		...	446	376	SSE	NW	11.59
Target Time—22 minutes							
Passage 4	...	...	408	361	NW	S	
Passage 5		...	410	337	SW	ESE	
Selective 1 Finish			451	329½	WNW	NNE	12.21

RELAXED SECTION from Selective 1 Finish to Selective Start 2. FUEL at 451½/331½. Approach SSW. Depart NNE. TAKE CARE AT JUNCTION WITH "A" ROAD. Hand in Time Card 1 to Reception Control.

[OVER

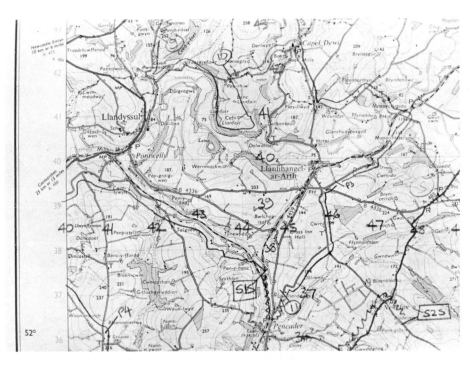

Route marking on a straightforward rally (Cilwendeg 1973). Note the way the route in this instance is pencilled on the left side with a zig-zag line on a liaison section. Note the marking of the map references up and along the map for quick plotting.

given in yards, for there might be any number of instructions that could be given within the space of a full tenth of a mile, and fractions of tenths are cumbersome. Road rally map reading is usually done in terms of the number of degrees in which the road changes direction, coupled with an indication of the severity of the bend, or junction. In this way a sharp 30 bend may well be slower than a long 90, but it is not for the navigator to command a driver to take a bend fast, as maps are never reliable enough for complete assurance.

You will see that the start of the first selective section in our example is at the junction with a private entrance to a farm. Actually when we arrive we find a queue of cars, since the previous section has been set at a relaxed schedule to allow breathless competitors time to regain their schedule. So when our time to leave comes up, we should be able to see which way the cars in front have gone, and heard the anguished tyres protest if a bend is deceptive on the map. The marshal hands us a card and reads out the seconds to our departure time, just as though we were astronauts. At the word 'Go' we face a 30 right and immediate sharp 90 left over the bridge and 30 right, then three hundred yards straight. Then we have a T-junction 90 left in front of a building over level crossing and immediate 90 right. You will note the approximate reference to a T-junction, rather than a fork. You are not certain that it is not a fork, but as a fork associates in the mind of the driver a slight turn, and as bad bends and obstacles follow immediately, it is best to give the severer instruction out of caution. The term 'T' means that you travel up the stem of the T. If we were travelling along the top of the T and wished to turn down the stem, the

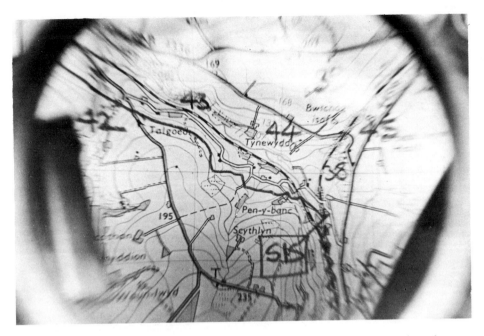

View through a map magnifier. There is no base on this magnifier. The distortion is of little practical inconvenience as the magnifier is always placed so you look through the middle, and it is moved across the map as you go.

instruction would be to 'Turn Off' to the left or right.

In our example we have to wait a third of a mile until we come to our first 'long' bend — in this case a long 90 right into a long 30 left and another half a mile or so before we come to a place that begins to defy easy description. When you cannot readily explain a feature on the map, tell the driver to ease off, whilst you collect your wits. The junction at 422 ½ 388 looks like a T-right and immediate single left, but if you study the map, you will note the way that our road turns into the junction. Because the roads are much wider on maps than in reality, you are on notice that things may be far from expected when you arrive. Maybe that the dotted white road on the left even forms part of one large cross-roads. Your warning to the driver should be

that you are approaching a junction from which, somehow, he must leave by the first exit on the right. Furthermore the complexity of the maps might mean that your innocuous slight left could well be much sharper. You cannot read maps with complete confidence. Even if you read them with absolute accuracy there is no saying that you will keep your driver on the road.

The essence of giving instruction is to convey what you mean to your driver in a way he will immediately understand correctly. Try where possible to use short words which cannot be confused. Nigel Raeburn used the term 'Take' when he wanted his road rally drivers to make a turn off the road. Keith Wood and Don Barrow before him used the expression 'Square' to mean a bad ninety-degree turn. Train yourself to read maps until you can read them in your sleep, except do not practise the sleeping bit on rallies. Practise until you do not have to think how you would describe a feature.

When you have mastered describing roads, concentrate on

It seldom hurts to check your route before a road event and often saves dropping a clanger! It is also a good idea to check with fellow co-drivers the times for each special stage. Kevin Gormley (left) with Lyn Jenkins.

describing land-marks. Land-marks are vital for two purposes. Firstly they convince a driver that you know where you are, and that a series of slight errors in describing bends are not so much your fault as the map's, secondly so you can pin-point a place where an instruction has to be implemented accurately. Choose land-marks with care, however! I well recall ending up rolling over and over in the snow with Tony Fowkes, and in the quietness of the aftermath discussing why it had all gone wrong. I had been waiting to pass an entrance before warning of a tricky left-hander to come. It was quite a few seconds after I said 'Ignore

entrance on left' before there was a big crash. It was a bad choice of land-mark. The entrance was there alright – deep under snow. My stupid fault for choosing a bad land-mark, Fowkes' stupid fault for not realising that the land-mark was a dodgy one!

If you ever saw Dave Kirkham flying around Wales with Mick Briant in his Escort in the late seventies or with Steve Hill in the early eighties you will know just how vital landmarks are. There is practically no place in Britain where you need a distance measuring device, like a Terratrip on a road rally. Practically every junction can be found by reference to a house, a bridge, some woods, an entrance, or by reference to the curve in the road. Suppose, on our map of the Cilwendeg selective section, you had wanted to turn off left just south of Passage Check 4, instead of going straight on south. The casual glance will tell you

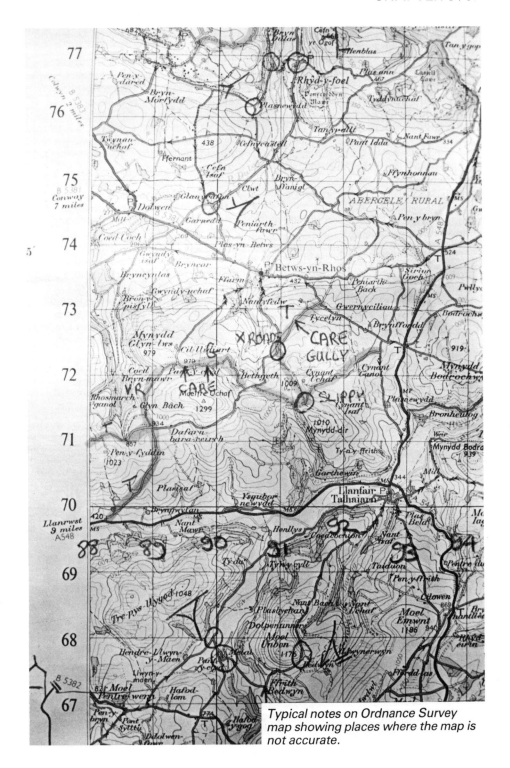

Typical notes on Ordnance Survey map showing places where the map is not accurate.

that the road is virtually straight, but close scrutiny will show that the turning is at the end of a slight curve. Such a curve will be easily visible to the driver. Alternatively, you could say that the entrance is opposite the end of the building on the right. It is less helpful to tell a driver that when he passes the track on the right he has gone too far!

Maps are the hub of a navigator's existence, but close to maps in importance are clocks. In theory the man who wins takes the least total time over a series of sections, which all sounds very simple. But it often happens that the fastest man does not

Control procedure; opinions differ as to whether it is quicker, and therefore better, to have your door opened or to expect marshals to sign your road book through an open window. Cars like the 'sliding window' Minis have windows which are tricky to open, and offer a small aperture once opened. This navigator is using a home-made magnifier. I hope he does not suck his pencil when the car is in motion!

win. I was navigating Barrie Malkin on a stage rally in the West Country, when we were fastest over the stages yet only came second. The reason was that our best time, at Brendon, was well under the bogey time, and the time of our rival Martin Clark was only just clear. As Martin beat us in total time on the other stages, our great advantage at Brendon was nullified and he won overall. Similarly Paul Faulkner and I were closely matched with Harold Morley and Peter Bryant on the 1972 Dubonnet, with Paul actually catching Harold after a series of controls. Unfortunately the minute hand flicked on to the following minute between Harold's entering that control and when Paul crossed the line, so that we gained no advantage. Later Harold went marginally quicker and gained a minute and won. These occurrences are commonplace, every navigator in the land can cry in his beer thinking about them. What they prove is that clocks and watches need careful attention in case they spoil your chances when your back is turned!

Back in the old days of sealed

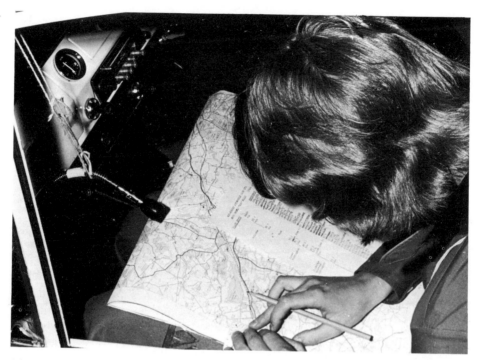

Ideal plotting pose. Note the way the navigator crosses off the points he has already plotted. Note also how the floppy maplight is restrained. The shorter form of maplights are generally better because they are more firm.

watches there were tricks you could play with watches. You could hold them at an angle so that the marshal would fall foul of the parellax bogey and read the wrong minute. Or if he looked a bright sort of bloke unable to fall for such a low trick you would helpfully shine your torch on the watch face — at such an angle that the shadow of the minute hand would fall in the wrong minute! Incredibly effective, that was! Nowadays the determined navigator will be unable to use such ploys, so he tries to leave a control ahead of the time the marshal put on the card — to give himself a head start time-wise for the section — or lure a marshal to put the wrong time down on the card. Usually one marshal holds a watch whilst another writes the time. Many minutes have been gained by the navigator repeating the time given by the watch-reading marshal, one minute wrong — and for the other marshal to write down that wrong minute. There are also, I might add, quite a number of navigators with cauliflower left ears, legacies of times when marshals have failed to fall for this ruse, and found a satisfying reprisal! This sort of thing is good sport. There are plenty of things that have been practised, such as wilful erasure of time cards, which go beyond the bounds of sport. You can never stop such things happening but whether the people who practise these things find the same satisfaction in rallying as we do seems doubtful.

Eventually you come to the end of your rally, which is where exercise number four in the obvious activities of the navigator comes into operation. This concerns the checking of results, and is perhaps naturally an aspect which receives the least attention. More rallies have been lost through casual attention by navigators to this aspect of their work than any other.

You have survived a long, hard mental battle through the night. Maybe you have achieved previously unattained levels of concentration and hardly made an error all night. As your driver swings into the forecourt of the finish garage or hotel, all you can think about is a five-minute nap. The five-minute nap turns into an hour-nap and apart from the disappointment of missing breakfast you run the danger of missing something far more vital — your chance of checking your penalties.

When you hand in your road books or your timecard as the case may be, make a note of the penalties you have incurred, so that as soon as your penalties are placed on the official results board you can check immediately to see if they are correct, and that they have added up your penalties right. Having done this and had the mistakes changed (or accounted for) your work must then divert to the business of checking the penalties of your rivals. If you have been running close to a particular rival you should have some idea of how he has been doing, assuming he has a competence with timekeeping. You will easily see whether his results appear to represent the sort of performance he was putting up, but if you are a novice and you do not know who is likely to be a particular rival, it is difficult to know whose performance you should be checking. It is even worse when there have been changes in the entry list and a person you happily assumed to have been in another class is in fact in your class. Mistakes occur in road rallying when a person's penalties are added wrongly — the first thing to check. They also occur when a person has gained an unaccountable advantage over you on a section that was severe. Maybe he gained an advantage because he lured a marshal into writing down a wwrong time. If this is thought to have happened, it is worth your while to raise a query in case an error can be traced and have the check sheets kept

by the marshals referred to. It could be that he left a control early or risked travelling the wrong way and his passage went undetected, in which case he gambled and won. He may well be less lucky next time! Once you have checked both your penalties and also those of your rivals, your job is far from complete, for you should next search for people who have put up similar performances to yours, but who suffered some heavy penalty at one place which set them back. These penalties could well be due to a mistake which is being corrected — leaving this person an unexpected rival. Maybe you do not notice that this penalty is being corrected before the time to raise a protest lapses — when you will be stuck with your lot. Maybe instead the penalty was incurred on a section that subsequently is cancelled. Some people have good luck in their rallying and this sort of thing happens to them. It never happens to you, though! Never discard the chances of people who lie behind you. On one rally (the 1968 Rallye Bristowe) we left the finish safe in the knowledge we had come a good sixth. The results were not finalised until some days later, when we ended up 14th. Our penalties were correct. All the others had errors in their penalties which were corrected and which put them ahead of us, but we had never in turn checked to see if they had compensating errors we should have complained about.

The problems mentioned above concern the usual difficulties that happen on timed-to-the-minute rallies. When selective sections are used a fresh set of difficulties can occur with results (and actually on the rally itself) and we will consider these in greater detail when we talk about stage rally techniques. In this respect, road rallying is much like stage rallying. Sometimes results of road rallies are not finalised after the conclusion of the competition, in other words after the results have been announced provisionally: they are finalised if

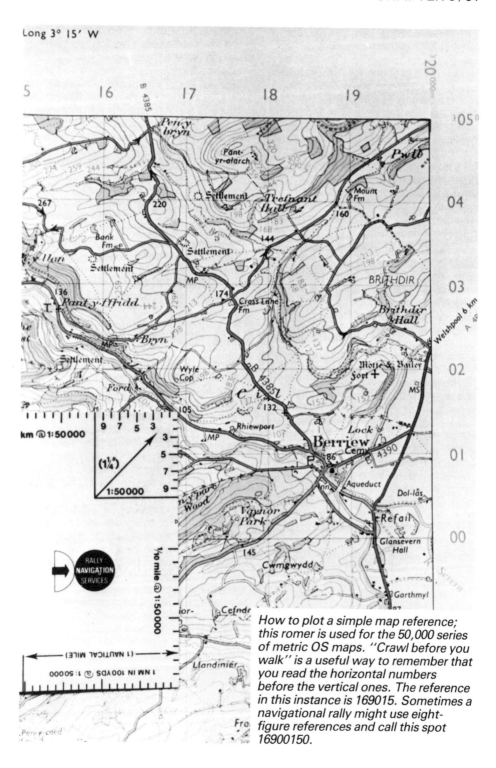

How to plot a simple map reference; this romer is used for the 50,000 series of metric OS maps. "Crawl before you walk" is a useful way to remember that you read the horizontal numbers before the vertical ones. The reference in this instance is 169015. Sometimes a navigational rally might use eight-figure references and call this spot 16900150.

protests are not received within a time limit. It is often better for an evil organiser not to publish the result at the end of the event but rather to send results out by post, for should a dispute lead to a protest then the organiser can dictate where the protest will be heard — and you can be certain they will not come to your home town for the purpose. One of the biggest bugbears of the sport is the results delay. It is bad enough not knowing who wins when you finish, but not to know that day inevitably means that outsiders lose any interest they might otherwise have.

How to have a mistake altered is a subject that needs mastering. The 'Blue Book' sets out the period during which a protest must be received, which is a half-hour if the results are announced within two hours of the finish of the competition (I have never actually found out what is the finish: the time the person concerned reached the end of the route? Reaches the end of the competitive sections? Whether it is the time the last person reaches these points? Whether it is the time the last person reaches them as extended by his permitted lateness? Or what?) or within seven days if the results are posted. The 'Blue Book' is most lax in the ruling, there is no obligation on organisers to display results — organisers are simply required to make available for inspection a copy of the provisional results. It is always assumed that where an organiser changes results that a further 'protest period' is required, but that is not mandatory.

As a navigator, your interests are to protect the interests of your driver and yourself within the bounds of sporting behaviour, and one of your objectives must be to conduct your affairs in a way to which the organisers concerned will be most likely to react favourably. This needs experience. Some organisers set themselves

against the sight of a protest bank note sticking out of your pocket, some would want to hush up any suggestion of their having made an error and turn against you if you broadcast your dissatisfaction. Some resolutely refuse to consider a point before the complete results have been worked — and then find that they have to re-calculate the lot all over again! There is no set rule about getting errors altered, it all depends on the people concerned. You must bear in mind that an organiser can ignore a request—even break a promise to have an error corrected, if you leave him to deal with it on an informal basis. If, however, you lay down your money and deliver the protest fee the matter has to be be considered, but cannot be considered until the results have been issued in full provisionally.

Tiredness and voluntary organisation are the two main root causes of trouble with results, both of which must be borne in mind if you are successfully to impress the organisers. Tiredness leads to reluctance to change results and a difficulty in understanding a different point of view. Volunteers get exasperated and lack concern for your plight, even sometimes they wonder why you cannot accept with grace the decision or intention of the people in charge of the rally.

In every aspect of navigating it is how you react to unexpected circumstances that makes you or breaks you. Everyone's popular image of a rally driver is that of a firebrand hero who is as mercurial in temperament as in his driving. A successful navigator is quite the opposite. It's the quiet men of navigating you need most to fear, people who say nothing unless it helps their cause, but who resolutely refuse to take no for an answer if they are in the right.

Chapter 6
History of stage rallying

The story of stage rallying differs from that of road rallying completely. Instead of being a topsy-like creation that grew, stage rallying shrank! The first special stage in this country was held on the 1960 International RAC Rally as a sprint across Scottish moorland, at Monument Hill. The tales of how Eric Carlsson's little Saab crashed and banged across the stage, and left all the rival crews foundering amid a shower of his stones and sparks will doubtless become one of the legends of the sport. Until then the RAC Rally had been a combination of road sections, like 'Mickey Mouse' affairs, races and speed tests. They were great fun for those who took part, but this was because of the occasion rather than the actual thing, and it was because the people did not know what better alternatives lay ahead.

The adventures of that little Saab set things happening, and in particular it spurred on a full blooded attack on Forestry Commission tracks. The forestry lands in this country were also being used on the International Scottish Rally, which previously had been a touring event attractive only to those keen on viewing the countryside

from open cars. The forest tracks were mystical in their effect, they represented a completely new world, yet were right in the midst of the country where we lived. They provided all the magic of a foreign rally without the need for going abroad, and even their toughness on cars provided little deterrent, as cars were easily retrieved and taken home. Driving through these forests was like driving in wonderland. You gould go for miles without sight of a house or a human being, the forests on hilly territory provided incredible vistas for navigators to enjoy. Perhaps more important than anything else it provided the chance of inoffensive rallying.

As soon as the success of forest rallying on the big home internationals (the Welsh Rally having soon joined the list of happy forest users, the London Motor Club London Rally soon coming along) had become obvious, a lot more people wanted to get in on the act. Already clubs had been scouring the local private land owners for permission to use their roads and tracks. When the possibility of general use of forestry territory was only just over the horizon, it seemed hardly worth while negotiating with

The little car driven by the big man who started the popularity of special-stage rallying in Britain. This picture shows Eric Carlsson in his two-stroke Saab on one of his last rallies.

successive individual private land owners. Furthermore, private land owners were seldom able to offer more than a mile or two of unrestricted track, the availability of Army land could seldom be guaranteed very far in advance, and road rallying was moulded so much in the idea of long, hard sections of two or three hours' length that one- or two-minute sections were quite out of keeping. Certain forests boasted great lengths of stage mileage. You could drive stage routes for thirty or forty minutes at Dovey, Kielder or Dalby and still not reach the end of them. Forests must be the answer, even if they had to be paid for at what seemed astronomical rates for repair.

There was another aspect, quite apart from the inoffensiveness of forest rallying that loomed large, and that was the increasing competitiveness of competition cars.

Even in 1962 or 1963 road rallies had to be set at 'illegal' averages in order that cars would be penalised without recourse to trickery of navigation, whereas the RAC MSA then permitted target averages of 50 miles an hour in the forests. With the loose surfaces, which in those days British drivers found more testing than tarmac, the set average was more difficult to achieve. The RAC realised all these things and eventually negotiated a scheme of allocations for forests which they introduced into the club rally world in the mid sixties. This allocation system was arranged through the club area associations, and unless you had special dispensation reserved only for major events, you could only arrange a forest rally if your association allowed you. In 1967 there was a feast of these events – the floodgates were opened wide – and every other *Motoring News* championship event went to the woods. But slowly the problems started to emerge.

The first main problem was the expense. In those days it was most unusual at club level to have a financial backer (entrants for rallying were almost unknown) and people gave up the sport insolvent. The entry fee covered the forest fees, but with the inadequacy of car preparation, cars very soon adopted a second-hand appearance, with failures in the structure which made it difficult to dispose of them through the trade. Furthermore sectors within the Forestry Commission soon cottoned on to ways in which they could thwart rallying. However many individual foresters enjoyed playing hosts to people who enjoyed their woods — and made use of them in an exciting way — it only took one individual with desk bound responsibilities who did

Special stages on club events started by being little extra features on road events rather than as a primary form of sport. Here Peter Noad and Mick Hayward tackle the Burrator Reservoir stage (a forerunner of the Water Authority stages used on the RAC Rally) on the 1965 Plymouth Rally.

not fancy extra work to annul the opportunities for motor sport within a wide range of forests. Obviously the forests of south-east England could not match the splendour of forests in Wales or Scotland, but then neither could the ordinary roads which rallies would alternatively have to use, but these forests were denied to clubs for this reason. The allocation system still exists, but often allocations are taken up and then not used so the availability of forests for the average club is much reduced. Often a club is given permission but then cannot run its event for other reasons. Through a further system of limiting the number of times individual forest roads are to be used a year, clubs then find the big events have taken the best roads and the smattering of small tracks available makes an event impracticable. In many ways the floodgates opened too quickly, and good things were sullied through overuse. Other things happened in this silly season however,

and these bode well for the future.

The rash of forest rallies taught a considerable number of lessons in car preparation, so that rallies based entirely on performance over non-tarmac surfaces were no longer anathema. Previously car preparation had been a most sketchy affair, and it had not been necessary for success. In the past you needed a navigator more skilled at the maps than your rival if you needed to win. Preparation had been basically preventative in nature; sumpshields protected the engine from damage, and so forth. Extensive work was ill-advised in any case, for rally cars were converted back to road cars when they were sold. Secondly the stage rallies that were held gradually demonstrated to competitors that good sport could be obtained within short, sharp sections, with easy liaison sections in between. It helped to wean competitors from disappointment at having concentration on competitive sections broken. This in turn helped road rallying which was under continuing pressure to ease the demands for tight sections all through a rally and introduce more relaxed

sections past highly built-up areas. Finally it opened up a completely new concept of rallying which was more sociable. From the financial aspect the rash of forest rallies brought home the importance of introducing money into the sport, none better than the Gulf-London Rally, which was perhaps one of the best enjoyed series of events on record. The major gimmick was a supply of free petrol — even the tax on the fuel was defrayed. Even in the mid sixties petrol cost was a major financial obstacle. Because of Gulf's Scandinavian connections, the Gulf-London rallies brought a large entry from abroad, and the arrival of these people, many of whom British drivers had never heard of, who promptly won the majority of prizes in turn gave a timely awakening. Just because established British drivers could drive

"Left anything behind, Paddy?" Paddy Hopkirk and Henry Liddon offer spectators a bonus in the form of tools falling from their works Mini. Although a Mini won the 1965 RAC, these cars were best known for their Monte Carlo Rally successes.

quickly, in their estimation, over the Abergwesyn moutain road did not make us a great rallying nation. Those Gulf-London rallies started a chain reaction that finally had its desired effect when Roger Clark won the 1972 International RAC Rally.

During this time another gradual process came about: the progressive erosion of importance of road rallies. Though it was often denied, it became apparent that no road rallies were being upgraded from restricted to national status (one of the main reasons, bearing in mind the 'adjusted' timing used, was the fact that a national required an RAC observer — who submitted a report back to Belgrave Square!). Existing events were being allowed to continue, and road sections were included in events counting towards the RAC national championship up till 1971. The bad national events became unpopular, the good ones were persuaded by leading drivers to drop the road sections, and the metamorphosis was complete. With an obvious emphasis on stage rallying and once the financial shock had died down, demand for entries in those leading stage rallies grew greater and greater, and when the events concerned could not accommodate the pressure for entries the only answer lay in having more events.

The need for 'more events' was something not as easily fulfilled as it sounded, for the only readily available venues which provided any length of competitive mileage were old airfields, and these were a far cry from the sort of rallying that the forests had started to popularise. Farm tracks were an extensively used remedy but, as previous experience had proved, the competitive mileage that they provided was limited, though the rapid change in surfaces on farm tracks gave them a special character of their own. They demanded a caution in driving greater than airfields, where the greatest harm that bad driving would normally incur was a spin. Farm tracks were invariably narrower, and often changed width

suddenly, with buildings or solid obstacles awaiting an errant car. The RAC International Rally, once again under the lead of Jack Kemsley who had guided it through many changes, offered two fresh approaches to the problem — the extensive land owned by stately homes and the often extensive land owned by water authorities. Many people thought that both these forms of stages were out of keeping with the strictly forest form of the International, but International rallying had always suffered a spectator problem; only enthusiasts spectated (which made the event one that was hard to justify to a potential sponsor, either for the club or for individual competitors) and those that did created havoc in the narrow approach roads to the forests themselves. There was enough rally mileage left in the RAC Rally to ensure that the basic character was unaltered.

Other than people like Jack Kemsley and Jim Porter on the RAC International Rally, and previously David Seigle-Morris on the Gulf-London Rally and Dave Stephenson of the old Castrol (nee, *Express and Star*) Rally, stage rallying has had few organisers with original ideas. Road rallies, however, seldom went through periods without a leader, thinkers like John Brown and Richard Harper, who were invited by various clubs to become clerk of the course, specifically for their ideas and their standards, although these events are now dying out. Gradually stage rallies shook off the road-rally thinking that had been adapted for the sake of example. Firstly the idea of sport at night became obsolete, and indeed the RAC International dropped the second successive night as being unnecessary. Apart from the saving of nuisance there was less need for electrical equipment (or even reliability), though cars still needed lights as they were compelled to use public roads for transit between stages, and had to comply with legal requirements. Secondly the concept of importance of

In the days when 'brute force' was more important than 'science', the Austin Healey 3000s did well. This is Timo Makinen and Mike Wood on the 1963 RAC International Rally. Eventually the Datsun 240Zs took over the big-car image when the 'old' BMC Team faded from competition.

arriving at particular points at given times became less vital than expected. Two reasons were responsible, firstly there was quite a feeling that having road timing as well as stage timing meant in many cases that a competitor was being penalised twice for a single delay: this was against RAC principles. If you are to be penalised twice, you will seek to drive harder than the permitted average dictates in order to save the second penalty. The second reason, applicable to the lower status events, was one of authorisation, as various authorisation requirements are waived if events are in no way competitive on road sections and if the route instructions do not dictate the route you take, or the time you take.

The only time instructions you are given in these events is to report to the stages within certain limits.

The reduced emphasis on road timing on stage rallies led to the increase in rally car servicing, (which forms a subject of its own later on in this book), which has gradually changed the face of rallying. This servicing aspect, together with the loosening of the road timing in turn started to change the tone of road rallying. Even in the early seventies, there were a hard core of enthusiasts who competed on both stage and road rallies, and ideas and techniques successful in one form of the sport still filtered through to the other. All the while other people were gradually being bred into stage rallying exclusively, almost unaware that any other sort of sport existed and certainly oblivious of the fund of knowledge of rally sport in general that road rallying provided. These people, who entered a rally like the Welsh, which even in the middle seventies required competitors to stay out of bed for two consecutive

"The hazards of spectating often go unappreciated by the people concerned". George Hill's Vauxhall suddenly throws up stones as it accelerates for the start line. Peter Russek Rally 1982.

nights, found themselves completely ill-equipped. In particular, they could not pace themselves. From time to time these drivers had the services of older navigators who remembered the lessons of years gone by and succeeded simply because someone else in their car knew how to overcome the problems of long-distance rallying.

With the BTRDA Gold Star series, which started in 1973, stage rallying at club level adopted the sort of consistency that *Motoring News* gave road rallying when it started its championship in the early sixties. In the case of the BTRDA, inclusion in a championship did not of itself give (at least to begin with) a guarantee of standards. It presented ideas within events and enabled good ideas to receive exposure to people of influence, people who would go away and organise small events in turn. It also included bad ideas and people could see for themselves why they were bad. In a lot of ways it was a crucible of stage rallies, through being a method of forcing up ordinary organisational standards.

All the time that the club drivers were having their own stage-rally sport developed the national level of rallying was growing. This middle course had

the RAC Rally championship as its central feature. Every established national event together with all the home internationals counted in this series, and slowly the standard of competition reached forward to amazingly high proportions. Roger Clark makes no secret of the fact that it was the constant practice in the national championship which provided his victory in the memorable 1972 RAC. Quite apart from familiarity with a lot of stages, for most forests used in the RAC route had at some time or other been used on an event counting towards the national championship within the previous year, the growing standard of the opposition kept him under pressure. There is nothing better designed to keep a person like Roger Clark on his toes than having a pack of young drivers all eager to beat him. And for these hungry young men there was no better carrot than having Roger Clark take your prize time and time again.

In 1977, a new RAC Rally Championship started. It brought together international status rallies under the little RAC Open Rally Championship. The RAC National Championship was retained but slipped a rung or two down the ladder of prestige.

The RAC Open National rally championship has developed the commercial aspect of the sport. This in turn has been to the advantage of most people. Club sport does not encourage commercialism in itself, for people at that level are grateful for every penny someone else offers, and will undersell themselves. People competing on International rallies cannot offer a regular exposure and so these events become a series of one-offs commercially. Back in 1974 a glimmer of financial hope came to the old National series when a group 1 category was introduced, spreading the prizes around a bit. All the while, however, the old championship needed the present engine-capacity class system that operates today, but there was not enough co-ordination between the RAC and the organising clubs, even at national level, for this to be possible. To stand a hope of success on the National level you need the best machinery. Even cars of marginally better specification can be far more expensive to run. A car like an Escort RS1600 2-litre costs considerably more, both in engine preparation and maintenance and tyre wear than a 1.7 litre RS1600, apart from the initial cost of stronger transmission parts. You need solid money to keep a reasonably competitive car running, and you need a competitive car to be anywhere near the chance of success. People like Tony Fowkes in the 1973 season drove an uncompetitive car with skill and guts in a way probably not seen in British rallying since Colin Malkin with his Imp in 1968 — and still he could only manage fifth. Those that beat him included Roger Clark, with a 2-litre Escort sponsored by Esso and supported by Dunlop, Jack Tordoff with a Porsche Carrera, a substantial motor trader sponsored by Ziebart, Adrian Boyd, 1.8 litre Escort, financed by Lombard and Ulster Finance and supported by R.E. Hamilton, a large Ford dealer, and Andrew Cowan (2-litre Escort) sponsored by *The Scotsman* newspaper. All better cars by far, in both specification and power. Tony was fortunate to have his Cables and Components support — substantial at that, but even so not sufficient to bridge the gap between fifth and first. In the mid-1970s foreign drivers became so interested in this old championship that they forsook their own national licences in order to acquire British licences and thus become eligible to score points. The Finnish driver, Ari Vatanen, won the National series in 1976 driving a works Ford Escort RS. The two current RAC Championships offer tremendous sport — for those who can afford it.

One-day special stage rallies take very much a standard form. The events start early in the morning — the bigger events usually on Saturdays and the smaller ones on Sundays — they include a total distance of 150-300 miles taking in ten to twenty stages. These stages are often held at individual venues for the most part, with perhaps some of the morning's stages duplicated later on. A bogey time is set for each stage, at 60 mph for loose surfaced stages and 70 for tarmac ones, bogeys which the organisers hope will not be attainable. Penalties are incurred by failing to attain the bogey time, individual penalties on each stage being added for the total penalty for the rally. As on road events, competitors are sent off from the start at minute intervals. It is this individuality of performance that characterises rallying from racing, although in road events more than one competitor is allowed to leave controls on the same minute.

Rallying is becoming more and more spectator orientated. We have televised Rallysprints, the RAC Open Championship is well covered by the media and even the RAC Rally has consented to 'spectator' special stages at racing circuits and stately homes, this all helps in making more people aware of the sport and in turn gives sponsors a return for their investments.

Chapter 7
Preparing for stage rallies

As with every other form of rallying the regulations are the starting point for preparation for a stage rally. The form of a stage event cannot differ in the same way as a road event, you do not have distinction between straightforward and navigational events, for instance. The main factor to consider is the anticipated level of competition. A co-promoted or a closed-stage rally will be at club level and as we have seen earlier, an event of restricted status can either be a local event, counting at best for an area association championship, or it can be a full-blooded national event in all save official status. The range of invited clubs will offer a guide should other pointers prove inconclusive. If a range of the leading clubs all over the country is offered, then you can draw your own conclusion as to the degree of opposition. If you keep a rally calendar it also pays to see whether the event clashes with any other, bigger, events, though the dates of races and other events which are not dependent on route authorisation, forestry allocation and heavy financial backing can be scheduled much earlier, and consequently there is less risk of a bad clash.

When you have assessed (in one minute flat!) whether the event is one for you, have a look at what classes are catered for. There is no standard set of classes at the moment, which means that your car might be a class winner one week-end and be lumped together with much more powerful cars next week-end. There is also a nasty little habit for organisers to merge classes should there be few contestants in one class, something which seems to be designed only to save organisers the cost of a cup. The supid thing is that people hardly ever enter for the cups! They sometimes enter in the hope of winning some money to defray their expenses, and most of all they enter for the glory of having proved themselves better than their rivals that day. One of the problems with rallies is that you have so few categories. There can be twenty winners in a day at Silverstone or Brands Hatch, and only one at a rally. At least a wide spread of engine classes means that there can be several 'winners' on a given event, which means that there is far greater satisfaction and justification in competing. There is sometimes an experience-category system, which is more relevant to road rallies than stage

The only time that navigators are not usually allowed in the cars is when there is a racing circuit test . . . Markku Alen driving a Ford Escort RS 1600 on the Llandow circuit during the 1974 International Welsh Rally.

rallies, whereby competitors are classed into experts, semi-experts, novices (or challengers), maybe even beginners. These classifications often differ from one event to another, maybe you need only to be eligible for a given class at the beginning of a season or alternatively at the beginning of the event itself.

Encouraging non-experts is difficult. Within the BTRDA Gold Star championship in 1973 and 1974, *Cars and Car Conversions* magazine ran a championship within a championship for people who could be considered amateurs, which worked well, for you were eligible if you enrolled and had not either succeeded in a BTRDA

event before or in an International. The successful competitors one year were not allowed to compete next year. A present day clubmans championship is the *Rallysport* series. The Scottish championship when run under Shell and *The Scotsman* newspaper also ran a 'challengers' category, which again depended on eligibility and enrolment. More overall control and standardisation would help, though such a system offers only an artificial classification at best, compared with an engine-capacity class system. Some events split up the entry in a way common with many autocrosses, by lumping together cars according to their design layout, such as front-wheel drive, front-engine rear drive and rear-engine cars. Some events split up classes further so that twin-cam cars are put into one class higher. It is quite a confused situation. To win a class on one event can mean little on the overall scene.

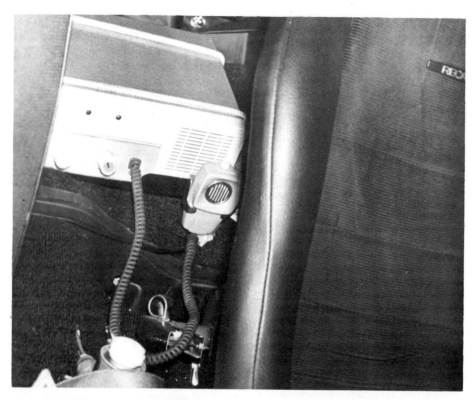

Two-way radio, here as fitted by the works Ford cars, so that service crews can be briefed in advance. This was an early version; nowadays lighter ones are available.

Every now and again an event does not restrict itself merely to the daylight hours, some starting in the middle of the night and running through to daylight, or the other way round. Some, particularly in the winter, are intended to be all-daylight events, but late numbers, especially if there has been a hold-up during the day, can find themselves having to tackle stages unexpectedly in the dark. Check this straight away and advise your driver so he can start ordering replacements for his broken spotlights in good time. Then check the length of the event, where it is to be held, what sort of stages it will use, how many miles of stages there will be, and what sort of surfaces. Organisers who are proud of their event will tell you all in their preface to the regulations — or if they forget they will tell you if you telephone. Beware the organiser who fails to give you a straight answer! Obviously many organisers have promised land-owners freedom from interference before the event, and will not give map-references, but at least they will tell you surfaces and general description. Have a peek at the acknowledgements in the regulations. 'The Defence Land Agent' means that Army land will be used. 'The Police Forces of . . .' tell you the authorities whose territories the rally will cross, which together with the list of required maps can easily rule out certain stages. The name of a garage may well signify that a halt will be there, which tells you in which direction the rally will proceed. Sometimes the name of a private landowner is given as well, and from previous rallies you might know which stage he controls! Sometimes permission is needed to cross private land to reach forest territory, so that grateful thanks in favour of 'Keeper Younger Botanic Gardens' means that the rally will use Loch Eck Side stage in Scotland. The information you gain in this way is for your private pleasure of anticipation, not for an excuse to make an unauthorised visit in advance. If your car is caught on land about to be used as a stage, the RAC MSA will soon have your competition licence off you as well! Remember many stage venues are made available only on a sporting, non-profit-making basis, so that trouble caused by you — even if nobody could prove that it happened — might turn the mind of the landowner concerned against rallying.

Rallies using special stages demand precautions in the nature of fire-proofing, the inclusion of roll cages and so forth. The regulations may not specifically remind you, stating solely that the event is open to any vehicle complying with RAC Vehicle Regulations. It is the driver's responsibility to ensure this is done, but a timely reminder may well save your sport for the day being ruined by trouble with the scrutineers. Next, look to see whether this event is one that needs full authorisation, which in turn means that there will be time limits on arriving at time controls and starts of stages. An event which has a half-hour lateness clause (like most present day events) is not an attractive proposition for a driver with a differential that is bound to fail! These are the main factors that need careful consideration before an entry is made but make your decision quickly as entries for good events are rapidly filled (time allowed: three minutes!). You will then sit back and think what you need to get for yourself and what you can be doing in order to help on the day.

In our chapter on preparing for road rallies we listed a number of useful objects which should turn you from being a sponger into a self-reliant navigator of use to your sponging driver. Some things which we listed in

Chapter 4 will not be needed on stage rallies. There is not the same importance on having the latest issue maps, unless it is a map which marks the actual stage and its approach roads. Sickness pills are less important for you will not be having to move your head up and down in a moving car so much, though if you are susceptible it is better to take them for a night stage event. Similarly a magnifier may not be essential, unless you reckon you can sensibly use one to read a map on a stage. The stopwatch comes into its own on a stage event for on stage events an official will always read GMT and you can check in advance whether the marshal is reading the time correctly. To see how this is done, read on quickly and wait until the next chapter. Cheap watches are fine until you come to a special stage, when they are prone to failure! Most digital watches have a stopwatch facility and some are even cheaper than a proper stopwatch, so there is no excuse for not being able to check a marshal's time.

Crash helmets are a subject by themselves, and the whole business of helmets is complicated by the intercom problem. Basically you want a hat that fits you comfortably and which complies with the RAC MSA rules. Not too tight or you will get a headache (and maybe break the sides of your glasses if your driver clouts you over the head in anger) or too loose in case it falls over your eyes when the car hits a solid bump, or your driver hits you over the head in despair. The intercom trouble is that there are several types of sets around, most of them need permanent fixture and you do not want to use a hat fitted with a speaker and ear pieces if you are going with a driver who does not have the same set. Some drivers keep a spare hat fitted with their brand of intercom attachment, with the speaker arm on the opposite side, either for the occasion when they drive a car with the steering on the opposite side or for use by a navigator. Such a hat is useful for a navigator with the same size head, but sadly navigators come in all shapes and sizes, and usually at either extreme. There is also the matter of professional navigator's pride. I do not want to wear a hat with someone else's name, there is always the problem of explaining to an angry marshal that you are not the man that spattered him with mud ten years ago at the start of the Dovey test, or worse still to a drunken Irish marshal that you were not the person who ran over his toes. Drivers are very sensitive over their identities. Chris Sclater refused to let me drive any more on a Circuit of Ireland when a proud father at the end of a long liaison section pointed me out to his son and said 'Look, boy, that's Chris Sclater'. Perhaps I was tactless in smiling back and not denying my true identity. Whatever helmet you wear, please make it look smart and professional. Do not leave it looking as if you borrowed it from a Hell's Angel, even if you did. Many navigators are turning to full face helmets, which are fine for stage rallies if you do not wish to yell a sudden instruction to a driver. Take heed from a luckless, rich but inexperienced Frenchman who once provided a car for Jean Ragnotti on condition he co-drive. Ragnotti's speed was a great surprise to this fellow and before long his stamina was beginning to weaken. Eventually his stomach could withstand the strain no more! — It is said that fellow nearly suffocated there and then, and never wore a full face helmet again. Full face helmets are even nicer than ordinary helmets for a little bit of signwriting and artwork.

Proper clothing is much more important on stage rallies than road events. For a start the event is likely to be in daylight and you need to look smarter. Then you are far more likely to have to lie underneath the car, push it out of muddy tracks or even walk across country to help. All these activities do little good for ordinary clothes. Finally the safety aspect. Proper overalls might just save your life or save you from painful injuries. Fortunately the RAC MSA is very well aware of the dangers of saloon car fires particularly after the Peter Procter fire in the early sixties and the Mark Ridout fire in the early seventies. There is very little halfway house in safety precautions. I remember watching back markers on a Donegal Rally after we ourselves had crashed. People wore full face helmets yet wore either a flimsy shirt or no shirt at all! Our car had been fitted with a proper bag-tank but I bet the cars that we saw were not. The trouble with rallying is that equipment all costs money, and heavy expenses do not go hand-in-hand with only occasional activity. At the risk of offering the RAC more power, surely it should lay down standards of safety and maybe even offer a non-profit making hire service?

It takes experience above all else before you can help a driver on a special stage, and experience is only gained by competing on that stage many times before. A little knowledge is worse than no knowledge at all, for loose-surface stage driving unlike tarmac driving demands a style which accepts the unexpected as normal. Your driver is expecting a sudden hairpin the other side of the brow. If you say *you think* the road is straight beyond a brow, or you have already made a wrong prediction you will upset your driver's style and make him slower than ever. What you want to aim at in a driver is instilling confidence. Help him to learn characteristics about each stage. Find out either from your previous experience or perhaps from knowledgeable friends little things about a venue. To say that a stage like Kilburn when tackled from the top of the hill starts with four hairpins will identify a stage to a driver. A driver who blindly drives for mile after mile without the countryside meaning anything to him will lack a lot of confidence. It adds a dimension of fun to him to see how reliable you or your informants are as well, so long as this

Always check with the regulations whether there will be night stages (Harold Morley's Porsche Carrera on the 1973 Cheltenham Festival Stages Rally) . . .

testing of information is restricted to general and not specific things. I once told Shekhar Mehta I thought that Minard was full of long straights, good 240Z stuff. After about three miles of constant corners, with the car nearly off the road on each, a hot and exhausted Mehta said he thought the source of my information was of poor quality. I did not dare tell him I had relied on my memory from two years previously. When questions of tyres are at stake a driver likes to make up his own mind but the navigator should

warn him of the characteristics of the stages. Chris Sclater was most wrought on the 1972 Welsh when we tackled a funny test that started on the tarmac ranges at Eppynt and went into the Crychan forest, on racing tyres. I did not warn Chris that this was partly tarmac and partly loose. We did a reasonable time, but I was not well respected for the rest of that night. All the pre-rally information I had obtained did not entitle me to make an ultimate decision.

Finding out in advance the surfaces of each stage is essential. If there are tests which demand racing tyres your driver does not want to know just one day beforehand. Furthermore if there will be stringent restrictions on servicing it is of little use for a driver to buy a set of racers if he would have to keep the same tyres on for another couple of loose tests. Getting used to your service crew and knowing their limitations in advance is also important. Some service teams include someone useless at driving and helpless with a spanner, but competent and reliable at finding his way. Sometimes you will not be blessed with anyone so useful. You do not want to discover ten minutes before you start that your service crew are unable to read a map, and should have left a half-hour before in any case. Furthermore you do not want to send a lumbering Bedford removal van full of foreigners across tight little lanes in central Wales, when it would be safer to miss one point and direct them along major roads. The choice of spares for the service car is clearly a matter for the driver to decide, but where you have more than one crew your driver will want to know if the people at the next service point are the ones with the spare differential or not. This sort of information is something you can learn in advance without waiting first for trouble.

At this stage it will be worth committing to memory some of the particular rules of your forthcoming event. Just as in road rallying there are various things that can be dealt with in alternative ways within the general rules of the sport. Try the following for starters:

1: Is there a maximum penalty for the stage? On British stage rallies it is almost impossible to find a rally without a maximum system, but the circumstances vary. The basic idea is to save a driver from incurring an impossible penalty for a slight mistake. Stage rallying is the excuse for driving with the abandon not possible when driving on the highway. A little error in sliding off the road on a corner can lead to a long recovery job. In such a sport it is sad if caution becomes the paramount requirement for concern. So what is done is to say you cannot

incur more than such and such a penalty, on one stage. If you do exceed your bogey time by more than that penalty, you only suffer that penalty instead of a greater penalty. There was a crazy mistake on the 1973 Chieftain Rally, when bogey time for a 9-minute airfield test was only 1½ minutes. Someone forgot that you had to lap the airfield several times. The maximum penalty was 500 points, in other words 8 minutes 20 seconds. If you look longer than 9 minutes 50 seconds you might as well cruise home in top gear and not trouble to drive quickly. I was navigating Russell Brookes in one of his Brooklyn Mexicos, and sadly we spun at the first corner, which upset my calculations that we might just beat the maximum. Usually one wonders if it is possible to beat the bogey! Just before the final corner of the last lap our maximum time came up, and we exceeded the maximum by fourteen seconds. There is more to this story which I will continue in our chapter on Clever Rallying, but suffice it to say here that the final watch was slightly inaccurate so that instead of a penalty of 8 minutes 34 seconds we were given 8 minutes 38 seconds, but supposing the watch was in error the other way, say we were given a penalty of 7 minutes 38 seconds. We would have felt sheepish if we had eased up. On a club rally remember that the marshal's watch is usually final, even if wrong.

Normally the results are based on another method. Your actual time can be taken for results purposes rather than your actual penalty. If you beat the bogey you still incur the bogey time, and there is no advantage to have gone as fast as you did. But in these cases there might be a maximum of perhaps 20 minutes. This means that on a short stage with a bogey of say 2 minutes, you will continue to lose penalties for another eighteen minutes. On the other hand on a long 12-minute stage, you will only keep incurring penalties for another 8 minutes. There is another aspect. If the bogey time is 2

. . . or whether any of the stages will be held on asphalt roads, which means you must take special tyres. Terry Kaby tackles such a stage at a deserted Army base in Hampshire.

minutes, it is fair to assume that even Hannu Mikkola will not complete the course in less than 2 ¼ minutes, and that on your first big stage rally you will be hard pressed to complete the course in under three minutes. The effect of the maximum penalty in this instance is if that you heave and strain at your rally car, axle-deep in mud for 17, rather than 18 minutes you might as well stop panicking to do the retrieval quickly and seek instead to do it properly. This is straightforward and obvious when you think about it. But what happens on a long stage? On the 12-minute stage, Mikkola for sake of argument will take 13 minutes 30 seconds, and you on a clear run (and forgetting a factor for getting tired, losing concentration etc) will take 18 minutes. The time you have to lose before your maximum will crop up is not 8 minutes as you might think but 2.

These calculations sound complicated, and so they are. But you must have a mastery of them before you can advise your fretting driver on what best course of action he should take. Any enquiry made when your driver is exerting superhuman effort to lift his car is bound to be terse, and your superhuman driver won't want a human waffle for a reply. He won't thank you if you let him sweat away when the attempt to save getting a maximum had long since become superfluous. You may still have an urgency to avoid arriving at the next control too late but that is our next matter.

2: What are the rules for arrival at controls? This is inextricably combined with:

3: What are the rules for delay allowances?

Luckily, most rallies now are run to target time. It is all explained in the 'Blue Book' but basically, it works like this: the sections, both stages and liaison, are treated individually, with a target time allocated to each — in the case of a stage, this target is in effect the bogey. These events are run with clocks set to BBC Time, so to find your due arrival time at the next control, it is a simple matter of adding the target time, usually a number of minutes, to the last time marked on your time card. Incidentally, it is becoming common for your start time for the next road section to be the same as the time you finished the stage, but discounting the seconds. So that if your stage finish time is 12:15:45s and the target time for the next road section is 13 minutes, your due time of arrival is 12:28. On arrival at a stage, you have two controls usually. The first is the Arrival Control, where you will be given a time of arrival at the end of the road section. The Second is the actual Stage Start. It is common that you will be allocated a start time by the Arrival Control which usually allows three minutes — to let you don helmets and generally start shaking with fear. In this way, if there is a delay for any reason, your time card is altered and as the section between Arrival Control and Stage Start is not subject to Target Time, your delay allowance is built in.

Then, there is of course a maximum permitted lateness as in road rallying, but it is usually 30 minutes and free of penalty. BUT if you exceed it, you risk exclusion.

It is also sometimes possible to arrive at a Main Control early under the three-quarter rule — even with Target Timing. The regulations will spell these things out for you, and you will need to know the answers off the cuff. When things go well and you have the time to work out the fine points, you won't need to know the answers. You only need to know the answers when things suddenly go wrong and desperation looms. The only time you have a breathing space for calculations is when you are driving to a service point. In case major work becomes necessary, it is always a good plan to work out two things: the maximum time you want to spend there, bearing in mind other features on the rally route to be encountered before the next time control, and the maximum time you can possibly spend, which assumes that you scrape into the next stage or control at maximum permitted lateness and drive as fast as is sensible in between. It is now popular however, to include service areas between a Service In and Service Out control, with a target time imposed between them. But the RAC Rally in particular is a modern day exception. It still includes servicing in certain areas only, as well as garages with prior permission, but they are not subject to their own target time, instead your servicing time has to come out of your road section target time. Consequently it turns into a fast road event as well. At the end of one RAC Rally a class winner was heard to remark, "it's not really a bad road rally, except for those relaxed sections through the forests!"

Rallies which do not need full authorisation have far less requirements for visiting stages and controls. The instructions will probably give a progressive opening time for each stage and control, and if you visit one stage within the times permitted, barring accidents, you will be able to visit the others within permitted times as well, even though you run well down the field from your starting number.

Check the lists of penalties to see if there is any provision for lateness at controls, other than exclusion. If there is, then be warned that some special control, maybe the first or perhaps the last, does not attract a special lateness penalty not applicable to the other time controls. Usually this is just a guide to stop you following too far behind schedule inadvertently, but just sometimes you have a penalty to

starting a stage earlier.

Know whether there are limits on servicing at certain areas, particularly at controls where there is to be a rest. It is silly to plan a major rebuild of your car when you and your driver are relaxing at a breakfast halt if you find your car is in 'parc ferme' all the while, and so servicing is forbidden. Together with this know the rules, if there be any, against replacement of various parts of the car. On internationals, watch carefully at scrutineering in case some of the parts are not marked and that exchange of those parts would go undiscovered.

Where there are special tests, like circuit races, study the rules with great care. If you studied the regulations for the 1974 Avon Motor Tour of Britain you would have found that it was far better not to complete a racetrack test if you had trouble, but simply to retire from the race. If you restarted and were running when the end of the race came, you would have your time and the number of laps you completed extrapolated upwards to the time you would have taken if you had completed the same number of laps as the winner and that would have landed you with a much higher penalty. There is a pretty golden rule in rallying. If something is unusual, think hard. There is bound to be an unconsidered loophole!

Make certain you know what you have to do to be classified as a finisher. The rules are usually pretty easy, but the apparent easiness of stage rallying has been the downfall of many.

You are now ready to go. The simplicity of stage rallying is an illusion. It means that a mistake can assume a far greater relevance than an error on a road rally, where organisers intend you to err. How will you fare?

Chapter 8
Stage rally techniques

As much as the excitement overrides every other impression, somehow the sight of a collection of stage-rally cars at the start of a daylight event is just a little incongruous. It is probably because they are completely out of context. At least a road rally car looks at home anywhere when it is dark, or simply getting dark. The lamps show that it means business. In the bright daylight a stage-rally car stands completely away from its environment, and its very stationary position shows up all its imperfections. For those in the know the excitement is undiminished. The mere sight of a sumpguard conjures up visions of the mechanical torture to come. The mere sight of those stickers calls to memory the cost of everything that will have to be replaced. And every person who religiously cleans his windscreen makes me wonder if that windscreen will be intact at the end of the day, indeed whether the car will look anything like a car at all!

In stage rallying a navigator is even more of a manager than he is in a road event, for a start there are more people he has to manage. He has at least one service crew, sometimes many more. He probably has friends

come to watch and who will want to know where they can go to see the action. With the increasing commercial interest in stage rallying as opposed to road rallying he will have sponsors and trade people eager to hear first hand what it is all about. There is a tradition in road rallying that the three of you, you, your driver and your car, battle away against the elements and the competition, and that is everything about the sport. In stage rallying the navigator is the co-ordinator of many different interests, all demanding attention and guidance at the self-same moment.

There is a considerable range of the degree of seriousness with which you can take stage rallying. The responsibilities of a navigator depend on this degree, so what we will do is to take the most basic responsibilities and gradually expand on these. Quite the most important job of a stage rally navigator is to ensure that the driver gets the results he deserves. Stated like that, it seems that the navigator is just a make-weight who has been given a job to justify his existence. But things are more involved than that. The number of rallies in which the wrong driver has won is amazing.

Cases are always hushed up to spare the feelings of the luckless man guilty of neglect. From time to time the true situation is not known to the people concerned, though often the rival crew has spotted was has happened and vested interest has preserved their silence.

Errors occur on two occasions: in the timing itself and in the results. If you let your driver down on either of these occasions, all the magic manoeuvres in the world will not retrieve your position. All stage rallies in Britain are now timed to the second. Generally speaking cars are sent off to tackle a stage at one minute intervals when the start clock reads a full minute, now and again cars may run at 30 second intervals on certain stages, starting on the full or half minute. Both start and finish clocks are set to GMT. This means that you will in either case be able to anticipate the reading of the finish clocks from the time-of-day clock or stopwatch you use. There is none of the road rally business of expecting watches to be set to times

that enable organisers to penalise you. Watches may obviously be a little out, and on occasion an isolated watch might be a long way out, but this will not be by design. If you carefully check that you are given the time at the beginning of the stage that the start clock reads when you start, you will always be able to avert an error. That, at least, is the theory. What goes wrong?

Firstly, you can forget to check the start watch. Very easily done when your mind strays on to other things, the attractive lady spectators, the car on fire right behind you, your driver who stalled the engine when you come under the orders of the marshal. Secondly you can forget to start your stopwatch. Thirdly either you inadvertently stop the watch in midstage or the watch stops itself.

Francesco Rossetti gives his driver Maurizio Verini every impression of falling asleep! He could not have been completely disillusioned, for they ended up as European Champions!

Both probably due to fright! Fourthly you become confused at the finish of the stage. If you use a stopwatch, theory requires that you calculate the time that the finish clock should read by adding the starting time to the time your stopwatch says you took over the stage. Maybe you forget the time when you started. Theory states that if your calculation does not accord within a second or two the time the marshal states you should, you should personally inspect the marshal's watch to ensure you are given the time the watch says. Sometimes the finish watch is held by the marshal who signs your timecard, when at worst inspection of the watch involves only a walk of a few yards. Assuming, of course, you can undo your belts quickly, that you untangle your intercom leads, that your stopwatch does not tangle with your belts, that you do not trip over the belts in your rush to get to the watch and fall face (and roadbook) down into mud, and lose your composure. But then the watch may be back at the flying finish, some fifty or hundred yards away. Most clocks are now electronic with digital readouts that can be frozen at your finish time, so checking is a simple matter.

These are some of the reasons why the simple job of checking times is not always done. The trouble with this business is that an error cannot easily be sorted out later. If you go at the end of a rally and ask an organiser to correct an error of a minute (for that will inevitably be the extent of the mistake) you will be derided by sceptical rivals who accuse you of trying to avoid the just reward for leaving the road and losing a minute and an organiser is bound to take the same attitude. You may swear upon your Blue Book that you are honest, and that the marshal will bear out what went wrong. But if a marshal is capable of making one mistake he has probably made several, and he will be damned if he can recall which cars were unlucky. That assumes, of course, that he had the courage to present himself at the finish and not gone home in disgust at competitors' manners. If a time is to be corrected, it has to be corrected at the time. The way to do this is use your nicest manner and point out how and why the error occurred and show what the correct reading should be. Unless you can do it just like this, the marshal will become flustered, be unable to think either quickly or correctly, and panic. A marshal's self-protective instincts insist that his judgement is right and that you must be wrong. It is not easy being a navigator on a stage rally — any more than it is being a marshal. At least a navigator has the thrill of competition to keep him interested. I only wish that stage navigators did not have to face this sort of thing for it does nobody any good.

Let's be charitable and say you got all your times right. You get to the finish and find things are wrong. You have not won! Why? Much of what you do at this stage is just the same as on road rallies. Whatever your driver does, your job is to hang around until the results are announced. You leave the crowded assembly area at your peril. The minute the results board is erected, it is surrounded by jostling crowds of ruthless navigators and self-interest drivers. It is almost your turn to panic. You have a half-hour (make a note of when the results are announced) to check everything. You have got to look everywhere at once! If you arm yourself with two things, your problem will be eased. Take an entry list, for often a results master sheet will refer just to competition numbers and not give names or types of car, then take the roadbook which lists the stages and in which you should have added for reference note of your penalties. As on a road rally, tackle your task in stages. First check your penalties and your total and see that they are right. Then check the people who have beaten you to your dismay: that is your class or personal rivals, or the winners if you are aiming at

```
8.27    25.94              S.P. A5 CORWEN
                           DO NOT SERVICE ANYWHERE ON A5 (POLICE INSTRUCT

6.39    32.33

0.23    32.56              S.P. DENBIGH

2.79    35.35              S.P. PENTRE LLYN CYMMER
        (0.51 TELEPHONE BOX)

1.13    36.48              STAGE 19 START                108(116)/978531
                           CLOCAENOG 1

4.10    40.58              STAGE 19 FINISH               108(116)/005534
        STOP ! RECORD TIME ! PROCEED IMMEDIATELY !
        NO SERVICE AFTER STAGE FINISH UNTIL AFTER TOTAL MILEAGE 54.11

0.07    40.65

0.13    40.78              STAGE 20 START                108(116)/006531
                           CLOCAENOG 2

8.20    48.98              STAGE 20 START                108(116)/038537
        STOP ! RECORD TIME ! PROCEED IMMEDIATELY !

        NO SERVICE AFTER STAGE FINISH UNTIL AFTER TOTAL MILEAGE 54.11
```

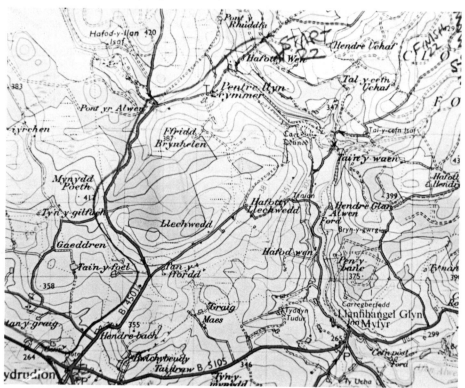

Top left: A typical international rally route card, showing the Tulip symbols with the interim mileages. This example comes from the 1974 Fram Castrol International Welsh Rally.

Bottom left: Please read this map in conjunction with the typical route instructions with which it corresponds. Note the way the route is pencilled by the side. Many navigators pencil the route both sides with arrows showing the direction to be taken, but if a navigator only draws a line on one specific side, say, to the left of the route, no arrows are necessary and much pencil work is avoided.

outright success. It is often tricky for you, amid the thronging mass, to check your rivals' totals, so often it is easier either to jot their penalties against your own or if you are simply interested in one person to compare times on a 'Plus 2 seconds, minus 4 seconds' basis from stage to stage, and see if the ultimate difference of the penalty is correct. Then your next job is to spot the people who put up similar performances to yours, but who appear to have had an isolated disastrous time on a stage and consequently are placed well down the field. This is to forestall a cancellation of that stage and then finding they leapfrog ahead of you. If you discover no errors, it had been a good rally. But rallies seldom work that way!

The most common error is a straightforward arithmetical one. An enquiry will have this corrected by the organisers — if they have provided a results enquiry facility. If they do not, you know the only way you can ensure your complaint will be noted — with a protest fee! The next common error is a competitor being given a minute. This is very easy to spot. A competitor can always lose a minute suddenly (he should have corrected this at the time if it was not genuinely incurred) but he cannot jump a minute on his rivals. An intelligent organiser will spot this immediately. He is always at liberty

simply to add another minute (or the relevant part of a minute if the fellow has been given a time which showed he beat the bogey to the penalty). Courtesy dictates that he should first inform the crew concerned in case they can show good cause. No competitor aware of his position will complain at having his lucky time put right.

The other errors that a results board will throw up are more fundamental. Things like late numbers putting up consistently faster times than early numbers. This could have occurred at a muddy, snowy or grassy stage that dried out in the passage of the rally — but it could also show that a watch had gone funny. Things like a midfield blockage caused by some outside circumstance. Only when the board is assembled can it be seen how many people have been affected, and can the organisers decide whether the circumstance is *force majeure*, that is something which is that person's bad luck, or whether the occurrence is so deep rooted in its effect that it would be fairer to cancel that stage.

Many organisers (the good ones!) put up a board at half-way and list penalties as and when crews surrender their first-half road books. These are unofficial results, but may at that time throw up problems which the organisers can consider whilst the second half of the event is in progress, and before they deal with the results of the second half. Let's hope that things are going well. What is next? Once a navigator is capable of the preventative aspects of his job, he can think about the more positive ones.

Constructive arrangement of service crews is the first objective for a positive navigator and is dealt with in Chapter 12. Then the next aim is to try to help a driver as much as possible. This takes many forms, the simplest ones first. Watching for arrows on a stage is the easiest. A driver on a stage concentrates on what is happening fifty yards ahead of the car. If he looks up into the distance he will lose

PASSAGEM N.º	CHEGADA ARRIVÉE ARRIVAL	H	M	S
		12	34	00

N.º 2-5 (0,6 km depois da EN 205)

19,6 km	Tempo)))))——→ Distância ←——((((	0	30	00
12-34	PARTIDA DÉPART DEPARTURE	12	04	00

N.º 2-4 (FAFE — 13.ª P. Classificação)

CONTROLES DE PASSAGEM

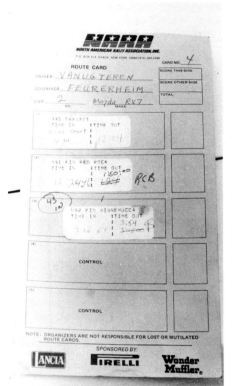

Two types of time card. Top is a
Continental card, which is designed to
fit a time printing machine, though (as
here) the time can be written in
personally. Opposite: An American
time card using a system popular in
California designed to reduce the
number of marshals.

concentration. Arrows are something
you can spot from afar, so tell your
driver what they say. On special stages
arrows appear at every junction, and
almost invariably a little way ahead of
each junction as well. On some stages
arrows also appear on bends, which is
sometimes confusing, for unless you
know they will be used for this purpose
you tend to slow and look for the
junction that is not there. Some arrows
indicate the severity of the impending
junction, others are placed at right
angles irrespective of the severity. The
pre-rally instructions should warn you
which style will be used: if they do not
it is worth seeking out the organiser
and finding out in advance. It saves a
time-consuming overshoot on the first
corner, if nothing else! The RAC MSA

now rules that a tulip diagram complete with distances is given for each stage, so if you use your distance trip properly, you can pinpoint every junction for your driver. If you can tell your driver what you interpret from the distant junction he will be prepared and maybe not bother himself to lift his eyes from the road to check. Arrows are not the only symbols you will find. There will be caution boards: sometimes an exclamation sign, sometimes the actual word. Sometimes these boards are placed alongside the hazard, sometimes a discreet distance beforehand. It is usually intended that roads you should not take have signs warning you of this, and organisers usually intend such junctions to have marshals to observe compliance. Not always are these things done, however, so always beware. Start worrying if there are no wheel tracks ahead of you. Start panicking if you come to a dead end! I came to a dead end in Radnor forest on the 1965 Welsh. We retraced our steps to find a marshal re-erecting the arrow that we never saw. This was *force*

majeure, for only we were concerned. If on small-stage rallies this happens, your best course is to inform the marshals at the finish and see if they will give you permission to have another run. If they substantiate what you say, your second time can count. If they cannot, your first time will count instead and you will be censured for cheek! This is less easy on bigger rallies, but the effect of such a delay on your position on a bigger rally will be less marked. Do not be too angry if you do not succeed in having another run, for strictly the RAC rules forbid re-runs.

Your next major job is to think of things all the time, and be completely

"Five, four, three . . ." Note the way that the navigator makes sure he can see the watch as the marshal counts the seconds. Many rally cars (like Rauno Aaltonen's shown here) are so noisy that the driver will not be able to hear the marshal and is relying on instructions from the navigator over the intercom or from seeing the official clock himself.

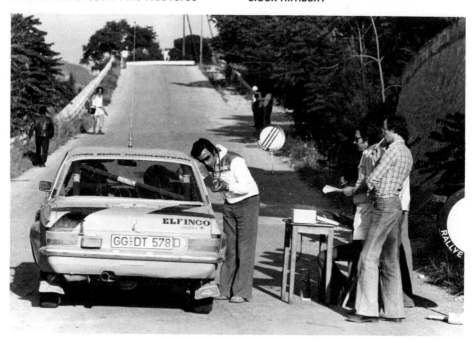

Navigators do not always have specific duties on stage, but on this occasion the crews were given Tulip arrow signs for the stage as well as road sections in between. This is to save having a stage cancelled should an arrow be blown down. Here the author checks that Chris Sclater was correct in turning left. RAC Rally 1978.

reliable in doing this! What a tall order! A driver can only give his best when his mind concentrates only on his job of driving. The biggest single act of thoughtlessness is running out of petrol. 'Absolutely simple', say the road rally fanatics who rate stage navigators as potato sacks. But they are used to standard cars that don't go wrong. They are used to cars where it isn't essential to have an intercom in order to make themselves heard. What a boring lot they are! They don't have bag tanks, double tanks, bigger tanks. They probably think that dipsticks are for measuring oil in sumps — never ever having seen a dry sump engine! Running out of petrol happens on countless occasions, and almost every

time a moment's thought by the navigator could have saved it happening.

The next thing is working out a starting procedure. Dust is a horrible obstacle, and uncomfortable as well. It is often possible to delay starting a stage in order to give the dust an extra minute to clear after the man in front has kicked it up. It is seldom that the second minute will not give you a clear passage. If the air is so still that it doesn't, then any amount of waiting will not materially improve the visibility. Drivers from the Safari and the Scottish tell terrible stories of dust, of the frustrations and dangers it causes. Never understimate it. It is far worse than fog, for fog drifts can clear within a hundred yards.

Following a route on a stage rally will always be pretty easy, at least by road-rallying standards. You will invariably have a Tulip road book and somewhere in it should be a list of map references as well. It always helps to plot your route on O.S. maps anyway. You can plan your service crews' cross-country routes, you can pick up

The flying finish location. You will see the marshal with his watch and his helper with the telephone line to the stop control.

where you are if you should find an error in the Tulip road book, or your Tripmaster fails. When you have plotted your route you can have a feel of the route and spot where the difficult sections lie. On longer events this is important, for you can see more easily the sections where you will be able to make good time and where it would help your driver's performance to rest and let you drive. You can easily spot which parts of the route pass through towns, providing you with slow progress. Develop a system of directing your driver and conveying route instructions in an almost insignificant manner, for this saves your energies and does not break up the concentration of your driver, whatever he is doing. Nothing is more aggravating than for a driver to be pouring out his miseries — or even be

trying out on you a funny story — to have you interrupt with something banal like 'Turn left at Traffic Lights, Signpost Wigan'. Unless you are one of those naturally amusing people who can hold their own in conversation at all levels of life, try to develop a habit of listening and sharing the interests of a driver. If he is keen on photography try to find out a few things about lenses, or at least get him to tell you things about his subject. It's amazing what drivers think about in rallies. Mike Hibbert drove along in complete silence for about a quarter-hour with me on a Welsh. He then said 'That girl young Sclater married, Sally. She's nice, isn't she!' For a man who had just that evening equalled Per Inge Walfridsson's time on a special stage I could not believe he was so far away from the thought of rallying. I asked him if he had been thinking of Sally all the while. He pondered for another fifteen seconds or so, and said 'Yes!'. Saving energy takes a conscious effort, and pays off. On a one-day

The time at the end of a special stage is taken when you cross the flying finish line. Your driver will then slow down and stop at the stop line which is where the marshals will note your time on the road book. At this point you must check that the time is correct.

event you can get quite tired by the finish at teatime. For the driver it is then time to relax, but at that time you have to be at your sharpest, ready for the inevitable free-for-all when the results are announced. On Internationals the matter is worse, for you need more stamina than the driver. He will go to sleep on liaison sections, and leave you to drive. Not much chance for you to nod off, for you have also to keep your wits about you on the stages as well.

The most advanced form of stage-rally navigating, is telling your driver about the stages themselves. The better the driver the less you need to worry about this. Timo Makinen once slid off the Penmachno stage on an RAC and stuck. His navigator was Henry Liddon and I was intrigued to know just how frightened Henry must have been, for at that stretch of the Penmachno stage there is one of the worst unguarded drops in Wales. I had been there a few months before and been staggered at the beauty of the

view and the nastiness of the drop. 'Not at all', the bespectacled master of the maps replied. But what about the drop? 'What drop?' he asked. Either he was a fearless robot, or as I suspect he did not know how dangerous it was. It was night time and foggy, and Timo does not go over edges, so why worry! Have you noticed, incidentally, just how many navigators have glasses? They also, all of them, have little holes in their brains that lets every drop of sense run out!

If your driver has a surname ending in 'en' he will have reactions so fast that he can escape damaging his car even if someone put a ten-storey house the other side of a blind corner. But this talent does not extend to the sort of drivers we navigate. For our drivers it really does help to know that a certain bend tightens up on you, and it certainly helps at times if you can say that the junction shown by an arrow to be ninety-right goes right back on itself. It is really nice to be able to tell a driver of something dangerous ahead. There is a nasty bend in Dalby, a forest full of very long straights that are pretty harmless save for the log piles beside the road and the humps. But one such straight goes out of keeping with all the others and goes into a long tightening curve. Even Mikkola went off here on an RAC once. It's interesting for a driver to know that he is just approaching Mikkola's bend. There is another corner in the same forest complex where another long straight suddenly swerves right, downhill, into the trees, with an escape road straight on. If you know exactly

LANARKSHIRE CAR CLUB LIMITED				CAR NO.	HOURS	MIN.	SEC.
MASTER CHECK SHEET			STAGE or CONTROL No. ....1.7....				
			STAGE - START or FINISH (Delete				
CAR NO.	HOURS	MIN.	SEC.	CAR NO.	HOURS	MIN.	SEC.
12	11 :	42 :	53			:	:
2	11 :	51 :	56			:	:
17	11 :	53 :	04			:	:
15	11 :	55 :	02			:	:
39	11 :	56 :	17			:	:
28	11 :	57 :	00			:	:
38	11 :	58 :	29			:	:
30	12 :	00 :	43			:	:
19	12 :	01 :	20			:	:
1	12 :	01 :	39			:	:
18	12 :	04 :	02			:	:
21	12 :	06 :	20			:	:
14	12 :	07 :	04			:	:
26	12 :	08 :	19			:	:
36	12 :	09 :	31			:	:
45	12 :	10 :	18			:	:
42	12 :	11 :	21			:	:
27	12 :	12 :	34			:	:
4	12 :	15 :	37			:	::

Above: The start and finish marshals keep check sheets which act primarily as a method of checking an ambiguous time card or road book entry. Note the way that the order of arrival can be other than the numbered order of competition. Also note that you can scan the list to see how rivals have done. This list shows the finish times and not the starting times. Practically always the starts will be at a 'whole minute' so reference to the second column tells you what you want to know. In this instance the fastest men were number 4 (Billy Coleman) and number 1 (Roger Clark). On a longer stage like this, the times of later drivers can be confusing as the sheet will not state the number of minutes they took.

where such a hazard lies you are extremely valuable to your driver, but if you do not you are worse than useless. You will slow your driver and get yourself in a stew from worry, neither of which is a good thing. The corners that catch out the real masters of the sport are usually the ones which marshals who lay out the course never really understand. At the speeds they drive when opening the course, there is no danger. They will put boards that will warn the clubmen of danger, but seldom warn of dangers that would catch out the experts. John Brown is a past master at squeezing extra speed from his drivers in Yorkshire; but he only calls the bends he knows to be accurate. Ian Grindrod is another map man trusted implicitly by drivers, as was Dave Richards before he retired.

Some stages can be read off the map, particularly the farm-track sort which you find on the day-stage events, although a piece of poor map-reading, when you are driving a stage with junctions arrowed and there is no chance of going wrong, is worse than none. If you can read the road well, a driver will use what you say to complement what he sees. He will not drive blind. The sort of situation in which map-reading pays is where you say the road curves a certain way and from looking at the road your driver would not have thought it did. Unless you know you can rely on your map, your map must be no more than a guide. Private roads and farm tracks are clearly less liable to be accurately portrayed on the maps than public roads, and in turn minor public roads can be wrongly portrayed on the maps after revision whereas major road changes are usually altered without delay.

One of the most striking developments in forest rallying in recent years has been the effort to make the best possible use of the surfaces of the stages, and co-drivers can help here to an enormous degree. The starting order in rallies is dictated by the results of the drivers in previous events, so apart from ensuring that your driver's record is faithfully explained to the organisers there is little more you can do, until you come

''He made the mistake, but I could have calmed him down!'' 1975 1000 Lakes Rally.

to the event concerned. On the forests, the matter of the starting order is of crucial importance. Hannu Mikkola once said that the difference between running first and second can be as high as two seconds a mile. Of course, the advantage between second and third, tenth and eleventh, thirtieth and thirty-first will diminish exponentially, but always that difference exists, except in a few special occasions like when the track is originally snow-covered, or if later drivers will have daylight. Nowadays, once a rally starts there begins a race to improve your starting order.

The regulations for the timing on rallies seems to change on every event, but in Britain, quite a common scheme is 'Target Timing'. This system is devised to ensure that you do not rush on public roads, but the effect is very interesting. It means that once you are ahead of the man in front, you stay ahead. Thus if you catch a driver on a stage and overtake him, then you will be due to the next control either one minute earlier — or at least on the same minute. In the latter case, then the accepted understanding that the first to arrive will start the next stage in front of any other driver who is due at the same time. The layout of the controls is as follows:

arrive at SF sometime during 15.32, maybe the first will be sent away from SD at 15.32 and the next at 15.33. The rules are not always the same.

Between SD and the following SA you have a specified time: maybe just a minimum time only or sometimes a precise time, earlier or later than which incurs a penalty. The time spent waiting between arrival control and stage start is "Dead" Time, *ie*, not counted at all — provided you are ready to start the stage on a marshal's instruction.

How do you get ahead of the man in front? Firstly by taking full advantage of the occasions when you arrive at the same minute, and being certain that you stay ahead on the road section that follows. Sometimes you can be cheeky to advantage, while in a queue for the start of a stage and overtake a car or two. The chance to jump the queue does not often happen, however, since normally the delay between arriving at the time control and leaving the stage start is only a couple of minutes. Furthermore, there is seldom a lot of room to squeeze past. Secondly, by precise and fast servicing when the distance between stages is very short and you have to change tyres in between. Thirdly, it is sometimes possible to take

SA	SS		SF	SD		SA	SS		SF	SD		
—	—		—	—			—	—		—		Special Stage
—	—		—	—		—	—		—	—		Dead Time
		—	—	—						—	—	Road Section

SA = Stage Arrival, SS = Stage Start, SF = Stage Finish, SD = Stage Departure.

Between every SS and SF, special stage timing applies. You arrive at the SF as soon as you can! Often SF and SD will be the same place, sometimes your time at SD will be the same time that your arrive at SF, *ie*, if your arrival time is 15h 32m 37s, your time away from SD will be 15.32. On other occasions it will be 15.33. If two drivers

advantage of other rules. On the 1979 Scottish Rally there was misguided permission to arrive at rest halts without penalty ahead of schedule. In addition it was stated that the order of departure from each rest halt would be the same as the order of arrival (obviously to make marshalling the cars easier). Nobody who saw the crazy neck-and-neck race between Pentti Airikkala and Hannu Mikkola up to the time control at Gatehouse of Fleet will forget the scene — nor the frenzied argument at the control afterwards.

Organisers using the 'Target' timing system often use rest halts to absorb any delays and close up the gaps in the field caused by retirements. Unfortunately this means that later numbers lose out on their rest and/or service halt. In fact at Teeside on the 1978 RAC the last 30 or so crews were clocked out as soon as they arrived, whereas the front runners had a two hour halt!

On occasion it is useful to delay as much as possible. During the 1977 Mintex Rally there was known to be snow at the Stang stage, and the time loss per mile when tackling a virgin snowy stage is far, far greater than the time benefit in driving on a virgin forest, and consequently the more delay that could justifiably be gained the better. Whereas the urge to jump the queue is human, the wish to let others past is less expected! Of course it is always possible to arrive late at a time control, but at best this means you are using up part of your permitted lateness whereas at worst you gain a penalty. But especially in dusty conditions it may be better to clock one minute late. In Brasil 1979, Walter Rohrl clocked in one minute late, and then found he was much quicker on the stages – even by more than the minute that he had lost – but that was when the more usual European system of time controls was used. This is as follows:

following road section. Thus if you lose a minute's road time you will stay an extra minute behind, whatever time you take on the stage irrespective of the driver in front. This system means that if you start each stage behind a slower driver you cannot get ahead. On the other hand it makes certain in advance the times the cars will start each stage. On the 1979 Portugal Rally, for many years voted the best organised rally in the world, only one out of 45 stages did not start exactly on time – and the delay was just one minute! The 'target timing' makes overall control very difficult. Every year the RAC Rally, which uses this system, faces problems. On the longer stages the later runners take so long that they cannot arrive as late at time controls as the early runners. To give the later runners a completely free chance to take advantage of the system, the marshals could never be given a time to close their controls!

There are plenty of schemes whereby you can gain an advantage – or sometimes deny the man behind an advantage he was wanting. In dusty conditions the following driver will want to wait as long as possible before starting the stage. It is a matter of great inconvenience for the person behind if you do not clock in exactly on the minute you require – but wait at the time control until the next minute almost arrives. Often dusty rallies are run with cars at two-minute intervals, especially after the first day when quite

SA	SS	SF	SA	SS	SF	SA	
–	–	–			–	–	*Special Stage*
–	–				–	–	*Dead Time*
–	–	–	–	–	–	–	*Road Section*

Here a different set of circumstances applies. There is no stage departure control: the road section starts at the moment you begin the stage and finishes when you arrive at the next stage. In this way when you drive quickly over a stage you give yourself more time to tackle the

a number of cars have retired. By hanging back you might be able to make the following man start only one minute later – especially if his co-driver is not alert enough to see what you have done.

The recent revolution within the world of watches has had a marked

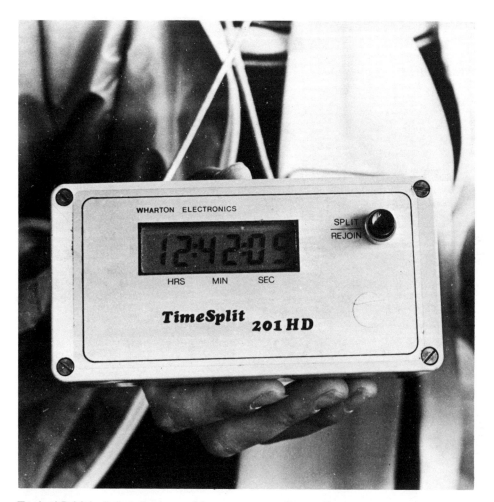

Typical British digital clock — with LCD for day use and LED for nighttime.

effect on rallying: indeed if any one thing has improved rallying standards, it must be our friend the digital display. Firstly the official watches can often be digital affairs with stop mechanisms built-in, and since these were introduced into rallies in Britain the number of cancellations of stages through misread times has fallen incredibly. Furthermore the reliability of these watches seems to have improved, so that cancellations for reasons of watch failure have also been reduced.

Secondly the computer results tabulation schemes have changed the need for checking results. You can assume that additions will be done correctly, but it is still important to check the individual times, for a computer is only as accurate as its programmer, and an error in programming the machine can be made. It is very easy for unusual penalties to be omitted: maybe the computer has not been programmed to cater for every possible penalty. Sometimes a penalty for one reason is entered into the computer as being a penalty for something else. The unhappy aspect of computer results is that you have to look all the time for

Opposite: A typical stage finish watch with split action second hand. The second hand has been frozen at 36 ½ seconds, whilst the other half continues to sweep onwards and is reading practically 54 seconds. 'Your' time is 11 hours 35 minutes 36 seconds. Both the other dials are of no consequence. You must learn to read these watches quickly and accurately for the marshal will want to flick the sweep hand back without delay.

Below: Two-way radios are now very much part of the competitor-service crew liaison. The author speaks to his crew whilst waiting at a time control, giving instructions as to the work to be carried out.

the odd things that might have gone wrong: in the old days of manual results you could easily anticipate what things would go wrong. Often competitors are completely confused because an unknown driver has been given an unexpectedly high position – often without ever gaining impressive special stage times, either! Eventually the cause is traced: one special time was not entered into the computer, so our friend's times are for one stage fewer than everyone else! This often happens when a time on a stage is being queried and has not been officially decided.

Another cause for strange hiccoughs in the computer machine happens on certain rallies, where they feed results into the computer in batches. Thus if you are running early in the field, you can gain interim results to which you are never entitled, since those results are limited to the first few results to be announced. Later runners (maybe they still have not even tackled

Code signs change each rally. Here is a good way to remember them.

the last stage involved) could easily have better scores. This is a particular hazard in the early stages, before a rest halt where the starting order is revised. The Swedish Rally, where it is difficult to alter the running order, has big trouble here.

Perhaps the best silicon chip development comes in the watches that you as a co-driver will have in a car. Firstly the days when you always had to walk to controls to check the official clocks is gone. It is a good idea to check the clocks when you can, but the accuracy of your wrist watch can suffice in an emergency. When waiting in a queue outside a time control, you can use your wrist watch to check when the cars in front are leaving, and this can serve as a check against the official watch – though be sure you are certain at what times your friends in front are due to check-in.

Secondly, at the beginning of stages, when nowadays there seem to be more things than ever on your mind (turning off the two-way radio, checking the intercom, tightening up your helmet, maybe adjusting your

Do not hurry away from a stage until you are absolutely happy with your time. However much your driver may be angry at having bent his car and be itching to rush away to a service crew to have the damage repaired, do not leave until you are happy with your time. Here is Geoff Loos at the end of the Epynt stage of the 1973 Gremlin Rally.

Never get out of your car too readily. If you slide off at a dodgy bend the odds are that there are quite sufficient spectators waiting for the thrill of getting you on your way again. If you unexpectedly jump out things might fall out through the door or you might have a more serious accident further on before you have fastened your belt up again.

facemask, gloves, maps or pacenotes) anything you can do in advance is worthwhile. For instance, if you observe the man in front, you can see exactly when the marshal lets him go. Then by studying your wristwatch you will be able to count down precisely the moment when the marshal will let you go. This means that you will not have to keep the window open and strain yourself to hear what he says, and you can safely wind up your window – one less thing to do when you leave. Best of all, however, is when the marshal will hold the watch so you can see it through your window, then you can rely on that instead of your watch.

Thirdly, you can check the times on special stages with greater ease. One problem is that only the very expensive watches have dual displays, so if you use your watch to help you countdown at the start, you cannot then use a single-display watch as a stop watch as well. Unfortunately the watch companies have not yet produced a watch with the most useful function: a mechanism to 'split' the time of day, however there is now a time/tripmeter on the British market that will do the job. This can also be done on the digital clocks used by marshals on British events. It's the old trouble: every time something is invented, you're never satisfied until something else follows it along!

When using maps, beware, the RAC MSA has set ideas on the matter. It banned 'marked' maps amid mounting pressure from foreign teams who were concerned about local knowledge during the 'secret' RAC Rally. After pressure from its own Rallies Committee, the situation in 1983 allows O.S. 1:50,000 maps to be used, but they can only indicate stage start and finish positions and the route along road sections. Forests must remain clear of markings. However, the rules only cover maps carried in the competing car, so it is possible to build up a pretty comprehensive stock of maps showing dangerous corners and deceptive firebreaks — if they are kept in the service halts, the information will, however, need to be committed to memory as 'notes' are not allowed to be carried in the rally car either. If tempted to carry items like these in the rally car DON'T — organisers do stop cars and search them regularly and the penalty is loss of competition licence for at least six months.

Successful adjustment to circumstances is the hallmark of a good stage navigator. There is the element of psychology in stage navigation which hardly ever enters into road rallying. Unless it is a matter of faulty car preparation, practically every retirement on a stage rally is one that a good navigator could have avoided. A driver crashes? Why? I remember that Peter McDowell had a big accident on the Isle of Wight in the late sixties. The reason it happened was that we had just suffered an annoying overshoot and Peter was angry with himself. Whose fault? His, probably. But who could have saved that accident happening by exerting a calming influence? Me, of course. A gearbox fails. Often an ailing gearbox or differential can be detected by a driver if he gives his mind to being receptive to these things. If the navigator had succeeded in freeing a driver's mind of irrelevant problems, would that failing gearbox have been

This is an instance where the navigator must jump out of the car. George Hill (Vauxhall Magnum) has reached the finish of the stage close behind the BLMC Mini of John Crosse. In moments like this it is particularly easy for you to be given the wrong time. The usual error is for the second car to be given a time one minute too slow. Here Keith Wood takes his helmet off after returning to the car having made certain his time was right. This occasion was on the 1974 Castrol '75' Rally.

spotted in advance? Have you ever noticed on those rally films the drivers saying they thought they would change a gearbox as a precaution? They never say they had time to think about the gearbox because the navigator gave them time to think about it, but that is the way it happens.

On a road rally a navigator succeeds on account of the things he does that nobody else does. On a stage rally a navigator succeeds on account of the things he prevents from

happening which will happen unchecked to other people. A most negative existence, you might think, but one a lot more important than is at first apparent.

"It is really good to be able to tell a driver of something dangerous ahead in time". This brow in Cairn Edward Forest hides a sudden right hand bend. The sight of the track in the distance is completely and dangerously misleading.

Chapter 9
Pacenotes

Pacenotes are the collection of symbols made by rally crews to enable them to know in advance the severity of the bends on a speed test on a rally. They are a specialised technique. Unless the crew can use them perfectly, it is better not to use them at all. They are designed to enable a driver to drive faster than he could drive by sight alone, a pretty dangerous thing. One missed instruction and you crash. Not only this but an immature rally driver with pacenotes acquires a headiness that makes his driving reckless. He suddenly finds he is driving faster than he has ever done before, faster than his reactions can cope with. It may be that the pacenotes work well but there are always the unexpected hazards lying in store that the notes do not warn about. These face a driver at a speed and a suddenness to which he is not accustomed and he cannot cope. A crash, with consequent delay and even possible retirement can result.

The antics of the works Minis in the mid-sixties captured the imagination of the motoring masses, and largely under the guidance of Stuart Turner these were greatly publicised and the whole pacenote business became immortalised. Pacenotes acquired the mystique common to any thing that is the province of professional or 'works' rallying. Club enthusiasts latched on to every scrap of information about these notes and immediately started to wonder how such notes could improve their own level of rallying. The thing that always gets forgotten in this sort of circumstance is that notes only help you when everything else has reached a pitch of perfection. It is like racing tyres, like left-foot braking and all the other mystical features you hear about.

Pacenotes are a system personal between driver and navigator. They can often be used in a common form which another driver can follow, but basically they are to enable one particular driver to attain speeds over a section that he could not otherwise achieve. Anything other than a personal system soon detracts from the benefit of having notes and makes the notes a waste of effort. It is often forgotten that the reason professional drivers travel so fast on notes is that they travel considerably faster than you or I even without them, and the notes only improve their times by a surprisingly small margin in

Navigators do not see much of the countryside when reading pacenotes. Phil Short misses the sights of Madeira whilst navigating John Taylor.

comparison. The notes have an added advantage in that a driver knows that there is far less likelihood of finding a nasty surprise just around the corner, so quite apart from the instructional aspect of the notes a driver will travel more quickly out of confidence alone. This is the confidence that is the undoing of an inexperienced driver. It is also the confidence that leads even to people like Markku Alen finding that if, on the 1000 Lakes Rally, a rock is left in the road where it does not belong, you crash into it instead of avoiding it.

The Manx Trophy, Manx Stages, Ulster International, parts of the 'Circuit' and some rallies using Epynt permit pacenotes to encourage entries from serious competitors, and the many accidents among the uninitiated, show that pacenotes *are* dangerous. In many events they are a necessary evil, to make a rally attractive to top-level drivers who would have no wish to

compete only to be beaten by unheard of local crews who happen to know the roads well. Leading drivers would never dream of entering an event like the Donegal unless notes were permitted.

Generally, in pacenotes there is a grading of corners along these lines: flat, slight, fast, fast K, bad, open hairpin, hairpin. The graduation of severity is self evident, but is also relative to the car's ability. An Opel Ascona 400 or even a Moskvich will know all about a bend that an 850 Mini never even noticed. Professional navigators have often noticed how even a year's development in a rally car's specification has made a difference to the severity of pacenote instructions. The term 'fast', you will notice, is the third grade down which is sometimes confusing. The term 'K' came into operation as a word which carries quite a sense of urgency about it, which is monosyllabic and which is not confused with any other word in the series. It represents a bend into which you have to take quite a bite, although the symbols indicate the relative speed rather than the number of degrees by which the bend will force you to change direction. An average 'K' bend would be a sixty-degree bend, in road rally language. Similarly a 'left' or 'right' would be about ninety degrees and a 'bad left' or 'bad right' about ninety or a little more, but for some reason or other demands special attention. An open hairpin is one which you can drive around easily, a plain hairpin is one which will occur invariably at a junction where your driver may have to use artificial means of spinning the car round.

This series of instructions is just one system. Many people use

Pacenotes come into their own when a driver cannot see which way the road goes or the other side of the brow. Here a Ford Escort Mexico comes within striking distance of the end of a stage at Epynt. Note the finish marshals in the distance. The man with the flag is at the flying finish, the group of people at the actual stop line. Tour of Britain 1974.

something pretty similar but excluding the 'K' and incorporating in its place the description 'medium'. Such a system often incorporates added variations, such as 'fast medium' and sometimes even goes to the extent of having a 'medium fast', something a little quicker than the 'fast medium'! Timo Makinen popularised the addition of the instruction 'maybe' after some bends — the meaning speaks for itself. Both series often have other conjunctives, like 'long', 'turn', 'tightens', 'very' and so forth. The 'turn' indicates that you will have to make a distinct turn off the route you would otherwise take. Both systems also incorporate various other features. Typical ones include 'jump', for when the car is expected to leave the ground over a bump, 'crest' indicating a place where you cannot see the road immediately the other side of a brow, 'keep' indicating which side of the road you should approach a brow, whilst there is quite a science in how the instructions are run together. There are five such methods. Firstly the offering of a distance of straight between instructions. Some drivers like to include every little hazard in their notes, not so much because they fear they will be embarrased if they do not know of that hazard, more to break up long distances in notes. The longer the distances, the easier it is to misjudge them, especially in bad weather. Secondly there is the full stop, which denotes a definite break between a sequence of instructions. Thirdly there is the ' + ' (pronounced 'and') and to show two instructions which must be taken together in a flowing manner. Fourthly there is the pair (or more) of instructions which follow very closely upon each other, much too close for neat racing style to come into play. Finally, a series of bends can be underlined to emphasise their closeness; this is an indication for the navigator to put effort in his reading to show the driver that more than customary attention should be paid!

Those previously mentioned are the usual symbols in the most frequently used types of pacenotes. There are other words or symbols used, to suit the occasion. The word 'to' shows that one bend turns into another, often in the manner of a simple curve turning into a sharp corner, and often an '!' will be useful for drawing attention, rather like underlining. Some people use landmarks freely, which I prefer, for landmarks enable you to find yourself in your notes should you lose your place. After a while you will not normally lose your place, but rallying is seldom normal. Without so much as a by-your-leave, your driver may command you to switch petrol tanks, switch on the windscreen wipers, fix a loose fire extinguisher, anything which takes your eyes from the notes. He will of his own accord slow down to a pace in which he can drive by sight while you are fulfilling his command, but he won't want you fretting about being unable to find the place again. Sometimes it is not really your fault you lose your place. Your driver might crash, and put you completely off your stroke. Drivers never say 'excuse me, we are about to crash, so make a note of where you have got to so you will not lose your place', they seldom even apologise for crashing. On one occasion we crashed off the road, and for the life of me I could not pick up my place again. I went completely to pieces! I later realised that we had regained the road two instructions further on. A liberal sprinkling of landmarks would help in these circumstances no end, so long as the landmarks you chose are immobile ones, and also can be seen at the time of day the notes will have to be used.

Making notes is an acquired art. Sometimes, especially for those inexperienced in making notes, it is good to start with someone else's notes and then modify them to your requirement. When you start on the brave new world of pacenoting you will have no idea what is 'fast' and what is 'K', particularly as you will probably

There are many forms of pacenotes and equally many forms of shorthand to record them. Here Alan Greenwood describes his notes to Paul White on Epynt army ranges, but Paul seems confused.

have to make your notes when the road is not closed to other users, and you cannot take a fast run at the corner to find out. It is a laborious job making notes from scratch. It needs bags of time. You drive slowly over the road with your driver calling out the instructions as he thinks they should be, then he has second thoughts about the last one, reverses a couple of hundred yards and drives over again to see if his original rating was right. Then he reckons that his estimate of distances was wrong, and wants to reverse again to have another look. Then he thinks just how fast his car will be going on the event itself, and goes back again to see if the distances should be shortened as a sort of special warning of the danger. At last you complete the stretch. Sometimes the test might be used in the opposite

direction as well, so round you go and start all over again. Sometimes it is used in only the one direction, so at least you have one uninterrupted journey for a change. Then you suddenly remember there was an alternative loop which ought to be noted, just in case the obvious route is blocked off, or you are commanded by arrows to go the long way round. Then you check your notes to see how they work. With luck you will not have to do so much reversing this time, but there will always be the awkard little stretch that completely fools you, and neither of you can work out just how it should be dealt with. On the third time, a well experienced note making crew should have got the hang of things. Then comes the practising, which you can only tackle if the roads are closed, and if practising is not forbidden in the regulations. Fortunately in many respects it is usual for British rallies to ban practising, but your notes will never be completely accurate unless they have been checked at rally speeds.

When the average organiser lays

"Fast left into . . . bridge". Pacenotes demand a special precision from both the driver and navigator. This happened on the 1976 Costa Brava Rally.

out a special stage he will never really understand about the things that make the real aces crash. It is similar with pacenoting. It is only at racing speeds that you discover the most serious problems. No driver is going to rely completely on notes made and checked at half-speed. And no driver is going to rely on notes absolutely when he has not had them read back to him at racing speeds. Reading notes, like making them, is an acquired art. Notes work the best when they enable a driver to drive in a flowing manner, and these involve working always some two or so instructions ahead. The flowing style does not come with a single advance instruction, or sometimes even with only two. The art is reading them so that the driver has always the optimum degree of advance warning all the time. There are other little things which help. Never let the driver fail to be aware when there is a straight stretch ahead. Finish off your string of instructions with the distance of the straight. This gives the driver an idea of how much boot he should give

the car on the final instruction before the straight. It is very easy to fall behind a driver. It is also very easy, unless you take proper care, to jump a line. With the complete reliance that your driver places in you, there is no room for error your end at all. Most navigators write instructions in bold type on every third line in a spring back notebook, in a bold hand — often with a black fibre tip pen. Wide margins should be used, and if you shuffle your thumbs down each margin there should never be any jumping a line. It means that you will be turning pages more than you would like, but that is small inconvenience. Buy a bigger note pad if you are worried! In the way that drivers never let go of their steering wheels, make certain you hold on to your pacenotes when you crash, so that when the banging and the crashing ends and the glass and dust have settled, you will be able to mark accurately which instruction went wrong. If, of course, you have not lost your pencil in all the confusion!

True pacenotes are of little use except on tarmac surfaces. In Britain the likelihood of noting loose surfaces is remote in the extreme, but continental events allow such practices. Drivers adopt a basic difference in style on loose-surface rallies and notes tend to be of the safety type rather than true pacenotes. If the loose-surface stages can be checked for their surface shortly before an event, to ensure it has not rutted and that nobody has placed a pile of logs in the wrong place, well and good, but things do not usually work that way. Usually there will be sudden puddles, a pile of logs that has slipped and sprawled halfway across the track, boulders just where your racing line would have taken you, and so on. These are the reasons why drivers adapt their style to one of anticipating the unexpected — and why pacenoting and the flowing style is no good. Loose-surface driving involves the car in a state of permanent imbalance, tarmac driving involves careful and perpetual balance. This situation works well in Britain, because access to forests is not permitted, so there is no temptation to go practising or even merely pacenoting in forests. The Army roads at Epynt are the finest places to go pacenoting in Britain, for except when the red flags are erected by the Army, access is unlimited. The opportunity to practice the notes at racing speed is denied because the roads are open. Unfortunately there are rules in most British International rallies stating that possession of pacenotes is evidence of practising, which is almost a contradiction in terms, and so a difficult and worrying crisis of conscience occurs. Sadly again, few club rallies get to use Epynt. There are also quite a number of good mountain roads used on road events where noting can be done: roads like the Abergwesyn to Tregaron road, the Tan Hill road, the Buttertubs road, the Dylife road, the Nant-y-Moch dam road. Each is several miles in length without any major diversion, which makes them even better for pacenoting because Epynt is quite a maze of roads which wind around each other and cause frantic changing of pages.

The types of notes I have described above are only a small section of the various ones being used. The very personal nature of notes means that everybody will tackle the notemaking system differently. Drivers like to keep charge of their notes, unlike a navigator who wants to keep the maps and the route cards: one driver's notes will not help another serious driver. Pacenotes are not the magic that clubmen think. They are the result of much hard work, and only then are of use when all the other circumstances are right. If you are starting your rallying career, please do not let this mystique get the better of you. You have a hundred and one things to get right before a single pace note will do you much good.

Chapter 10
International events

Once upon a time, the only way you could break free of the stranglehold of road rallying was to enter a rally abroad, and find out the things about rallying you never dreamed existed. Foreign rallying, in many ways, was the only good rallying you could find, even though it was an expensive and a lonely exercise. Such brave antics made you a hero back home. If you got to the start you did well. If you finished it was amazing. If you did well you must have been a member of a works' team! At home in those days there were just the RAC and the Scottish Internationals (the Circuit of Ireland being a navigational event in the main), the nationals were road events, and that was it. Now the scene has changed completely. We have regular home Internationals (i.e. RAC, Scottish, Circuit of Ireland, Manx, Mintex, Welsh and Ulster), we have national rallies that for their heat of competition could be called Internationals in any other country, we have clubmen going abroad for rallies simply in the hope that they can, for a change, catch a glimpse of the prizes! There are many internationals abroad that are well worth doing, which many drivers like to enter as holidays, but

there is no longer the *need* to go abroad. Those who aim at being professional rallymen need to enter foreign events, simply to give themselves the breadth of experience, but clubmen who aim merely at good sport have all the sport they need in Britain.

Internationals, be they at home or abroad, are characterised by the amount of advanced planning that they demand. Usually they are longer events which in itself makes the planning more intricate and aspects such as finance need more careful attention. Budgets for national events follow much the same format as restricted events and can be reasonably accurately assumed beforehand. International rally budgets need to be assessed with care. The headings which need calculating are as follows:

Entry Fee, (if competing abroad, include fee for visa from the RAC MSA).
Travel, to and from, both rally car (unless trailed) and service cars (petrol as well as ferries).
Hotels and Food for you, your driver and your service crew.

The magic of foreign rallying! This is Sandro Munari's Lancia Stratos on the Monte Carlo Rally in 1976 at the head of the queue.

Insurance, for rally car, for legal requirements, for personal accident.
Miscellaneous extras: photographs, drinks, souvenirs.
Maps, for you and your service crew.
Tyres, if tarmac rally, check if 100% tarmac route.

Carnet, for taking spares out of the country — obtainable from Chamber of Commerce.
Reserve for unforeseen eventualities (especially the cost of dealing with unexpected mechanical trouble).

Practice is a long and lonely business so the chance to chat to fellow competitors is welcome. Here Mario Mannucci, Shekhar Mehta and Sandro Munari (l to r) pause near the village of Upega in Italy.

Most of these items can be calculated with precision, though it is always sensible to speak to someone who has tackled the event you have in mind on a previous occasion, to see what unexpected financial shocks they discovered and how much petrol will be used in practising. It is unwise to rely on discounts for travel, for it is traditionally difficult to find the person who is able to offer such favours, and often there are hidden snags as to when such discounts have to be taken up, which particular ferries could be used to them, and so forth. Some foreign events are so keen to take foreign competitors that entry fees are waived, and sometimes free accommodation is offered. You can rely on the entry waiver if you have the offer in writing, but be wary of free

accommodation in case this involves staying with the organiser's great aunt who cannot speak your language, wants you in by 9.30 every evening and lives 25 miles away. If accommodation is offered, check for how long, for how many, and whether food is included. Do not rely on anything else! To find someone who has done the rally in previous years, look up the reports of the event in the motoring weeklies, and contact the people concerned. It may mean following up several leads to find the person concerned, but a few phone calls are better than a financial disaster that might put you out of rallying for a year.

The reason I have elaborated so much on the financial aspect in this instance is that so much is at stake, that if your driver underestimates things badly it will be you that suffers. In the final chapter we will talk about money matters generally. It pays to ensure your driver knows what he is taking on, for your peace of mind. It is possible to cut down on very few aspects. You need hotels local to the

Evening time on the Rally of Portugal 1982.

start, so you can always reach your rally car or the rally headquarters on your feet without needing friends to run and fetch for you. Taxis won't exist when you want them, friends will get side-tracked and will keep you waiting when you need them punctually. If you have ready access to rally headquarters, you will be on hand when results are announced, and notices which concern you are posted, and you will not have to get up any earlier in the morning of the rally than you need.

When a navigator knows a proposed International rally is a viable proposition, it pays him to undertake as much of the planning as he can. However organised a driver may be, he will have as his prior concern the preparation of his car and the service car. There will be items of equipment that have to be fetched and the increasing urgency of the event will take away from the driver his concentration on detailed planning. Even if he plans the arrangements he will want you to take charge of the paperwork relating to them and to know all about them, so why not do the job yourself? Hotels get booked up the quickest. Best to book first and enquire the rates afterwards. You can always cancel if you cannot afford them. There is a hideous ploy on some rallies for organisers to book a whole hotel, making everyone stay

Cars are often placed by the organisers of major rallies in parc ferme *before the start and/or at certain rest halts. This enables the cars to be marshalled efficiently and sometimes to ensure that competitors have the chance to rest and to make themselves fit to continue. No work is allowed in a* parc ferme.

elsewhere. Make certain you book at the nearest one to headquarters. Most hotels will give you street plans on request. Of all the arrangements, try not to be involved in your driver's insurance problems. The only insurance which concerns you is personal accident cover which you can deal with yourself. If you need help, the organisers will usually be more than eager to give you advice.

Planning ahead is the keynote for International rallying, even more than ordinary rallying. This happens in many ways, not the least that of conserving energies for the moment they are needed. Usually the first time a navigator needs to drive on an event will be on an International, and to me

the joy of driving a really super rally car — even if it is just driving from one stage to another — is one of the best parts about the sport. These are cars that you would never dream of owning yourself — sometimes cars that even limitless money could never buy. But the joy must be contained for your driving is not a perk, it is all part of your responsibility of thinking of everything in advance, of saving your driver's energies for when they are needed. This is one of the really few times when a navigator finds his job easier if he has also driven on rallies himself. It is a far from uncommon reason for retirement on a long event when a navigator crashes the car. This is terrible for the sport and for that navigator's reputation in particular. There are many navigators who find driving on the big events the opportunity they have always wanted to show their drivers how good they are. A driver looks for just one thing when he hands over his precious wheel. He wants to go to sleep and know he will wake up at the start of the next stage refreshed, and that he can leave everything to you

Under a flood of light in balmy air the rally is started. This is typical of a European International Rally.

in the meantime. Unless he can have this confidence, you are of little use to him. If you ride in an ordinary car with a good driver, one thing you will notice — just how smoothly he drives. This is what you should strive to emulate. If you are in a hurry to reach the next control, it is probably your fault that you did not restrict the time spent on the car at the previous service point.

With so much more to deal with than on a restricted or national rally, try to tackle everything as far in advance as you can. On International rallies you will usually be able to secure details of the route several days in advance. On British Internationals information packs containing the route details can be purchased for the service crews. On British rallies, save for a limited number of exceptions, it is not possible to reconnoitre the competitive sections of

the route in advance, so having the route in advance is an ideal opportunity to plan your service arrangements carefully. There may be the isolated cancelled stage, but at least when the service packs are issued the times of arrival at controls and the majority of stage details will be settled. The service packs on British events sometimes include a full road book, usually with instructions in both Tulip form and with map references for precise location of the actual stages. On foreign events the intended route is often included as a supplement to the actual regulations, by listing route numbers and towns to be visited, and sometimes even a map. To enable competitors to make their reconnaissance and pacenotes, the complete route is generally made available just over a month before the rally.

But before you ever come to set out on a recce for a foreign event — and particularly before you come to

Control procedure on foreign rallies is very much like that of British rallies except that controls are usually in the middle of villages and that the crowds are controlled by the police. This crew is having its timecard marked at the end of a special stage; in these circumstances the navigator does not have to leave the car as he might at a time control.

A control clock which punches the time on a time card is in common use on the Continent. Note the digital time accurate to the second. The time card is slid through the slit under the word "Longines" and the punch is operated by a button by the navigator at the second he wants.

collect your service pack for a British stage International — you must have given yourself as much time as possible to master the regulations. In previous chapters you will recall that the regulations have been the starting point for club rallies. So they are for Internationals, and even more so! The reason that regulations are even more important on Internationals is that International rallies have to comply with the relevant country's regulations as well as those set out in the *FIA Yellow Book*. The *'Blue Book'* has almost no relevance on even British Internationals. About the only relevance it has concerns permitted advertising. The first thing that you will note in International regulations is reference to the FIA homologation

forms. In practically every International your car must conform with forms of recognition for your model. These forms are available through the national clubs for the country which produced the car you are driving. Firstly they confirm that your model is Internationally acceptable for competition with certain groups, and secondly they state the special extras that can be fitted in addition to the modifications allowed under the standing International rules. Ensuring that your car complies with these rules is in your driver's province, but timely reminders from you will save your sport from ruin lest your driver be forbidden from starting through ineligibility.

The second factor you will note in the regulations is the need for an International licence, obtainable from your national club upon evidence that you have sufficient experience at lower levels of competition to warrant competition at the level you are now aiming at. Third thing that may be strange to you — and certainly will be strange the first time you go abroad —

Time controls on Continental events usuall demand that navigators leap out to clock in. Here the navigator is waiting for the time clock to show the minute that he wants before having his timecard punched with that time and then proceeding. Note the round international sign by the control desk and the sign in the road beyond which marks the extent of the control area. Servicing is forbidden.

Is it because the car is damaged — or that the co-driver cannot stand the pace any more?

is the system of marking. Gone out of the window are your pre-conceived ideas about not catching up lateness to avoid further penalty, indeed about not being penalised more than once for one delay. These foreigners have ideas of their own! Target timing is generally used, but with slight differences — instead of being timed from the finish of the previous stage, road sections may be timed from the start of the previous stage and usually time for servicing is not allowed for either.

One factor that is common to all Internationals is the importance of the class system. In the fifties and the sixties there was quite a crisis of conscience in rallying that the man in the little car did not have the same chance of outright success as the man in the big car. Sometimes national issues were at stake, particularly in France, where maybe a leading manufacturer only had little cars to rally, and obviously it was bad for national prestige not to give him every chance of winning. Well, that is now gone. They fiddle things in other ways! The emphasis is on the fastest cars, and smaller cars have honour in their classes. What is very difficult is keeping track on how other competitors are faring when you are in the middle of a class struggle in a rally. Firstly you can never rely on the official entry list, for there are often late changes in entry before the start, and scrutineering will discover cars in the wrong classes as well. Then the organisers are usually so keen on working out who is leading overall that they forget just how seriously you are taking your class battle and only after night halts do you get to know how you are faring — and sometimes not even then. For all that, the class system is important, especially from the commercial point of view. The more people who can win something, the more commercial interest can be justified. Maybe you will not like group 2 Sunbeams beating you, especially when your chances of buying one are limited, but factory Talbot involvement

is good for anyone rallying their cars. They know the answers to the problems you will face, and if the works team did not rally cars that are a little special much of the factory participation could not be justified, and ultimately you would be a loser. One of the BTRDA championship rounds saw Escort cars in the top twenty-two places. That would never have happened if Fords did not find out all the snags on behalf of the private entrants and it was consequently so easy to rally an Escort.

There is a further aspect to this class business, and that concerns the bonus system, by which if a driver wins some prize that has found its place on to a schedule in the manufacturer's competition department, you may well find that you are eligible for a bonus payment. Whenever you win your class on an International your driver should contact the manufacturer and indeed all the makers of auxiliary equipment and suppliers. Not all will help, maybe none at all, but the telephone call or telex will always be noted. It will be at least a little flag waving, and it will be surprising if it does not result in favourable supply rates for parts or equipment in the future. In the same way that you as navigator should always keep check on class rivals during an event, your use will be greatly appreciated if you remember to help your driver capitalise on any success you gain. Sometimes, particularly with oil produce, your driver will be asked to sign a written contract — little more than a duplicated sheet of paper — before you start. You can imagine that claiming allegiance to a particular oil after the event is open to abuse, and it is to introduce a little solemnity that these contracts are drawn up. Before you sign your allegiance away, read what the contract says and work out what you get back. Do you get free oil? Even if you have cracked your sump and want 100 gallons? In what position in class do you have to finish before you benefit? Then before you sign any

Ari Vatanen's Rothman's Escort RS was jointly sponsored by Rothmans and Castrol, but on this event local laws required that cigarette names had to be blanked out.

trade contract, look to see if there is a rival company offering contracts. Usually on Internationals you have two companies (say Castrol and Shell), and seldom do their terms agree. With one company your driver might get a much bigger bonus for winning a class and nothing for a class place. Your driver takes his choice and signs the appropriate contract. Immediate advice to the company concerned is vital, for the company's only interest in your result is to be able to advertise your success and that benefit has vanished the morning after. This is why I want you to know about these arrangements, for the morning after the event will be very full in the life of your driver, and it is he who benefits from the bonus in the end.

So far as equipment for Inter-nationals is concerned, this depends very much upon the sort of event. On home internationals there is little extra that you as a navigator will need apart from some sunglasses and maybe an old tatty pillow. Some document case is most useful, particularly if you are travelling abroad, something you can keep safely by your side — and even under your pillow at nights. Much of your equipment depends on the sort of event you are tackling and the country it is in. But this is not half as thorny a problem as deciding what event you should tackle in the first place. Once upon a time it was all too simple. You had to do the Alpine, followed by the Acropolis. You must drive a Mini, and if you finished on both you would be assured of a friendly handshake from Stuart Turner. That, in those days, was the ultimate reward, unless you were a Finn! We have our own range of Internationals, which in the case of the RAC, Scottish and Welsh are basically forest events. If you want to try your hand at a home International and blind tarmac roads there is the Circuit of Ireland, and if you wish to go the whole hog and trust your life to pacenotes there is the Ulster or, of course, the Isle of Man.

From there, we have all manner of directions in which we can point. If we only want to mix with people who speak English we have the Irish events and the Dutch ones. If we want the chance of winning money, there is little to beat the various International events in Belgium or Northern France. If we want to find out how the Finns come to run circles around us (or at least round everyone except Tony Pond) we can go to Scandinavia. Things to avoid are events that demand extensive reconnaissance and servicing, events like the Monte Carlo Rally, for instance. If we do not want to be far from home, there are many events not far from the English Channel. When planning a rally, always try to make your venture coincide with someone else from this country rallying a similar car. Not only will you not be alone, but there will inevitably be considerably more interest from the organisers and from dealers should your model of car be sold in that part. If you want heavy drinking sessions, there is little to beat rallying in Ireland!

Rallying abroad these days makes for a nice holiday, a change, a chance to see something new. No longer is it the only way you can find some serious rallying, however, as we have all we need in Britain.

Chapter 11
Going professional

Few things can be more attractive on the outside than being paid to do something you enjoy, even more so when the alternative is that you would actually have to pay! Going professional is a big step in any occupation, and rallying is no exception. At the risk of discovering the difficulties and disillusionment, we have the chance now of seeing what it really involves, and whether the moment of glory is really worth the months of trouble. There is one big problem with British professional rallying: there are very few opportunities for the occupation to be fulltime. This means that any professional rallyist — and a co-driver in particular, must expect to carry out a considerable number of other activities apart from sitting in training and rally cars. This also means that there is no need for a team to employ fulltime people — again in particular co-drivers. It is quite easy for a team to employ a person to sit in their rally car in his or her spare time. Furthermore, there are plenty of skilled enthusiasts who would do this without payment at all — and hence what opportunity to work as a co-driver there ever was is diminished! Nearly all this arises simply because

British rallies themselves are weekend activities. At least drivers have an increasing testing responsibility, but the co-driver has no pacenotes to make or lengthy travelling to undertake.

The majority of professional co-driving openings in Britain lie either with the elite of British teams who have rally programmes abroad, where reconnaissance is necessary, or in co-ordinating work within the rally departments themselves. Often this will involve a lot of desk work making plans — and often other work like representing the company, arranging forums, dealing with marketing of specialist components and so forth. Clearly the moments when you sit in your works-entered car are to be treasured, so before we speak about the agonies, lets dwell on the pleasures.

Firstly, professional rallying gives you the chance to do things a lot better than you could do privately. Remember the old adage, true in Britain if not so much elsewhere, that you are paid to lose and you pay for the chance to win. In what ways do you get the opportunity of doing better? Let's think about car equipment. The

"Professional rallying gives you the chance to do things better". In this case, the choice of tyres for use on the next stage.

car has all the equipment that a private team must accept. So long as you know your mind, you will get your electronic trip meter and your cars will have two-way radio fitted. Your seatbelts will be new, your cars will often be new as well — and every time they build a new car some of the old annoying inadequacies will have been removed. And when you get new problems, you will have the advantage of advice and practical help from experienced people. Having so many people involved with your activities is one of the most striking aspects you will notice.

When you come to the actual planning of the events, you have an added advantage again. The threshold of compromise is pushed back. You only need to say you will want to rest in a bed for two hours at a neutralisation halt during an event, and it will be arranged. When you work fulltime in a

team, you have the chance of concentrating much more on what you are doing. All the time you are two steps ahead of where you were back in the bad old days. Your planning takes on a new dimension. You become positive in your approach. Service planning is preventative rather than reparatory. All the little extra things you had wished for in your planning previously you can expect to arrange. When you had thought how nice it would be to know in advance what the weather was like on the other side of the mountain, now you have time to find someone who can tell you. So you can safely use dry tyres instead of compromising with intermediates, for instance. Slowly you begin to understand a lot of things about rallying which pressure — and often blind prejudice — had obscured before. You realise why professional drivers usually win. Professionals do not win simply because they are better drivers, they win because private drivers cannot organise themselves in a way which allows them to win. In due course, it means that professionals

New equipment is one great advantage for professional co-drivers. This is Ilkka Kivimaki in his works Fiat Abarth 131.

concentrate more on their driving, thereby giving them a further benefit.

Secondly, a co-driver's job demands more aptitude on the management than the participational level, through the increase in the number of people involved. You are now guiding a battalion as against a mere company of troops. This gives a wonderful sense of satisfaction. From your previous knowledge and experience, you can work out the number of service vehicles and the sort of functions they will perform — and leave other people to produce them. In British rallying the number of mechanics needed is never very great, so compromises seldom operate. The

Privateers have little chance of winning rallies like the 1000 Lakes in Finland. This is Arne Hertz and Hannu Mikkola enjoying the moment of Mikkola's record sixth win.

beauty is that you will have exactly what people you need. The change in emphasis between the preventative and the remedial work means that you will soon become the master of juggling with tyre-loading lists. You must calculate which vehicles will go where, which type of tyres — or how many replacement tyres — will be needed at the points where that vehicle will attend—and consequently when that vehicle sets off after liaising with the tyre base, which types and how many of each it should take. Funnily enough, one of the most common groans from drivers is "I did not have the right tyres'' — and in most occasions this means that he did not have the choice of tyre available that he wanted. And that often means something else altogether, that the co-driver did not calculate correctly which tyres should have been loaded on to the van in question! Of course there are many drivers who happily change their minds about which tyres they will want on which stage — and nothing throws out your carefully laid plans so much as that!

There is seldom a shortage of people who will run errands for you when you are working in a works team. Many times there are very good reasons why too many outsiders should not be attached to a team, but still even if a team does not allow you to employ any extra personnel, at least your fee means that you can personally arrange for someone to run these errands at your expense. Even if your team will not give you as much leeway as you would like (and the longer you are involved, the more that seems to be so) at least you have so much more financial freedom compared with those "bad old days". The people around you teach you so much more about your rallying than you ever thought possible. It is so easy to enter a team for the first time thinking you know it all (and indeed there are plenty of things that you will know better: you would not have been invited unless there was), but you soon discover whole areas that you knew nothing about — and never knew existed. Marketing people, development liaison engineers at the factory, professional publicity personnel, skilled mechanics — these are only some of the people you will come across for the first time. All this adds up to a new sense of fun: you are no longer competing just for your personal satisfaction. All these people are willing you on, are prepared to help you even beyond the call of duty, many of them become friends, and stay friends long after your term of duty with that team comes to an end.

You earn money in different ways.

Each team seems to work in its special way. With some you are a fulltime salaried employee, with others you are paid by the day. On some contracts you pass all your expenses (reasonably incurred) on to the team, with others only your travelling is provided, and another sum called 'day money' is paid in order to cover the many miscellaneous payments required (hotels, phonecalls, meals, etc.) — so a frugal existence gives you a few extra pounds. On some occasions your money comes direct from your driver, who is hired to present a complete package — driver plus co-driver. It may be the custom for crews to share the prize money earned, after a deduction for the mechanics. In some teams it is the practice to hold all the prize money and then distribute this at the end of the season (hoping that it has not depreciated too much in the meantime!). Obviously you keep a far closer check on how you spend your money, and you soon learn the ways of saving money, like not phoning from hotel rooms and checking carefully your hotel bills. Any time your accommodation is booked by a company, the bigger the company the better, hotel staff regard you as fair game for adding their private phonecalls to your bill and generally looking for increased profits. In many countries it is the practice for petrol attendants or waiters to ask how much you want the receipt made out for, hoping that your windfall will lead to a gratuity.

Obviously you come to handle a lot of money, much of which is not yours at all. This is particularly the case when you rally abroad. There are a lot of hidden advantages in this, but against this the risk of losing the cash or — just as seriously — your receipts, makes you cautious. Teams know how much rallies will cost them, and since many team managers were once competitors like you, they know how you can acquire money which is not from your entitlement. When you are such an asset to a team that financial

Sometimes professional teams carry out their work in real style!

indiscretions must be overlooked, you are very lucky, but you also make enemies and people are looking anxiously for the day when you can be dispensed with. There is very little loyalty in rallying at a professional level — certainly loyalty for its own sake. There are many ways of earning an extra buck in this sport without having actively to defraud your team.

Your services are often not required for long periods at a time, so the most important thing for you is to have another occupation or business, which you can turn to when you are at home. Finding one which you can leave at the drop of a hat is not easy, and often another occupation within the sport itself, such as being a journalist, leads to conflicts which can only harm your sporting ambitions. As we have mentioned earlier, much of British rallying works the other way round: your primary occupation is something else. It is the uncertainty of what will happen which is one of the worst aspects of professional rallying life. Even when you have a set programme at the beginning of the year, you will be very lucky if that programme will remain intact. Sometimes you are lucky and you get an extra event. One of the most important Vauxhall results in 1977 was second place at Galway, and that was a last-minute decision made after I had tentatively agreed to ride with someone else for that occasion. But on the other hand things can go unexpectedly wrong at short notice as well. The Vauxhall engine crisis in 1978 completely disrupted the programme, leading to several cancelled fixtures. So how can you be sure of what you are going to let yourself in for?

Inevitably you will make a contract when you start to work for a team. A contract does not have to be a parchment document prepared by lawyers, it can be a simple letter and even an agreement by word of mouth. Sometimes, an agreement can even be assumed through circumstances. Always the problem with verbal agreements is evidence as to what has been agreed, and this is the main purpose of a contract. Never think of a contract as the method by which you can require someone to do something. In rallying, by the time that relations have deteriorated to that effect, your position on the team is valueless and there are plenty of ways that your contract can be legally sidestepped without any satisfaction to you. It is a much more devious thing. It is a much more effective document to stop you doing something, as any formula 1 fan will tell you. But that is the stuff for superstars rather than you and I. So you want a letter, as much as anything to evidence what they are going to pay you and for what, setting out exactly

what you have agreed. Remember that it may be a good idea to agree a minimum payment for a season, in case everything goes wrong and the team does not compete on the events they had hoped. But the best drawn contract in the world does not give you rides when plans get changed. All it can do is get you some money.

Already we have been mentioning some of the problems that will affect you in your professional career, so while we are gloomy, lets look at them all! One of the biggest surprises you will have in a rally team is how much aggro goes on, much of which is never known about outside the team. Nothing brings a team together like success, but for every successful team there are two or three which are not successful, and that immediately breeds discontent. This is one reason why the drivers change teams so much. If this is a surprise, stop and remember that in any competitive sport, only one thing matters and that is winning. Much of the trouble is caused by people being ambitious: ambitious for themselves as well as simply for winning. These people do not even have to be drivers to cause trouble. Any team is a hotbed of intrigue, of people who succeed through intrigue and others who lose. Those who last the longest in this business are the cleverest. This aggro takes other forms as well, not the least being the constant changes of plans. Some teams are understanding in this respect, others are completely ruthless. And one of the greatest casualties in this uncertainty will be your family. When you were a privateer, your plans might go wrong for some visible reason, in professional teams they can and will go wrong for many other reasons besides.

The next problem is dealing with fools. In nearly every team (happily not *every* team) I have been in there has been someone there who comes under my definition of a 'fool'. Usually they are people for whom the team is one great ego trip — or worse still an ego

For every moment of success, there is a moment of agony. In this picture former Audi Team Manager Walter Treser explains to Michele Mouton, Mikkola and Hertz why their Audis were excluded from the 1981 Acropolis Rally.

trip for that person's wife. It is nice to travel and see the world, to boast about your journeys to your neighbours, but a rally team is no place for this. The job of a team is to win, but life is not so simple. No team exists without some bureaucrat having to give consent, and it is the appeasement of these people which has led to any number of jobs for professional drivers and co-drivers. In the way that the means by which successes are obtained on rallies is seldom queried, all that really matters to a team is that it exists, which means that someone has been persuaded into sanctioning the budget. Many times people go a 'second mile' within corporations in support of the sport: one of Tony Pond's most important victories was financed by an executive who exceeded his authority — and who ultimately gained full appreciation, but who could just have

easily lost his job. But much more often a team is sanctioned for all the wrong reasons.

Having accepted that these people have to exist if we are going to get our work in a rally car, having to live and work with them can be even harder. Happily not all will interfere, but some do to an embarrassing degree. Sometimes they demand jobs for members of their family — often very keen and entertaining people — but inexperienced and a liability to the team. Then interference can be even more harmful. One such person asked an organiser of an international event if it was true we would be excluded, without asking us first. Without knowing our situation, the organiser said he imagined we would, whereupon our friend went home and it was some time before he could eventually be contacted and told we had not been excluded and had won our class. To succeed despite all this is part of the game, and no doubt one of the reasons why we have to be paid. A private driver is his own master, but a professional driver is always at someone's beck and call. The most burdensome is an interview for the press when your mind is full of your immediate work. The worst part is that the threat of being branded as 'unco-operative' is very real. The very people who will sanction your employment are those who are very receptive to this sort of thing. One of the most important knacks is to impress the right people, but that is true everywhere in life. There have been extremely able co-drivers who have been banished by teams because they are argumentative and trouble-makers. Even though they have come to teams through connections with drivers, those drivers can sometimes have their jobs threatened by *your* behaviour.

How can you get into a team? Nearly everyone arrives in a team because of his association with a promising driver. Sometimes a team has a resident co-driver whom the team will wish to put with 'your' man, but it is rare indeed for a driver always to stay with one team: soon he will be on the move again and then he will be able to take you. Of all your aims, a firm relationship with one driver is the most important when looking for openings at the professional level. In due course you will develop your own identity, in the way you did when you started rallying in the first place. In my case nearly every team I have worked for arose from an invitation by the driver involved, and the same has gone for other co-drivers as well. Once you are in a team you make your own opportunities. Team managers seldom regard anything except your immediate suitability, so never regard your first time as your only one. You will be on the move at the end of the year — and maybe quite a bit sooner.

The Grand Prix driver Alan Jones once said that Christmas is the worst period of the year, and this is true for rally men as well as racing drivers. Until you know who you will be driving for the following year — and what events you will do — you are never settled, and this uncertainty preys on you. Unfortunately it is worst at Christmas

time. You get unsettled by stories in the weekly magazines, which hint at wonderful plans for your rivals, who you know have half your aptitude for the tasks involved. In my opinion few motorsport journalists know the peril of the word 'will', and whenever you see *Autosporting* and *Motor News* say that John Smith *will* co-drive during the next season, you can be assured that it will go wrong before long. In addition to depressing you it makes life very difficult for John Smith himself. Often his negotiations have not be settled, yet such an announcement slams the door on other opportunities. The best deals are those which do not get the banner headlines. Journalists often feel that they dictate the course of events through their writing. This is far from the truth, except insofar as things they have written ruin many alternative possibilities and often leave the published stories as the only remaining possibilities. At club level, the motoring magazines perform a great service, but often the inexperience of the journalists offers little at the professional end of the sport.

Enjoying the worship bestowed on you by your less fortunate friends is one of the best features of professional rallying. You have to be lucky to get into a winning team and not be snowed under in the incessant gloom which haunts so many others. Furthermore the life of professional rallying is seldom a path to riches, although the opportunity to travel, the excitement of being driven in (and occasionally actually driving) cars that soon become real live classics in their field and of course those moments of delight when success finally comes your way are the benefits. It is an experience not to miss. If you turn down a chance to compete with a professional team you will never forgive yourself. Your sport will not have been complete.

Chapter 12
Service crews

One of the nicest ways in which rallying has changed in the past few years is the way that so many more people take an interest in what you do. You have your driver, and with the advent of the day-time rallies many more friends come and watch what you do. You have sponsors and in turn they mean that local papers get involved. These people like to follow your activities, share your successes and sympathise when things do not go well. But in addition to all these you have your service crews, folk who often come to help you completely voluntarily. Not only are they with you all the way, but also they learn many things about rallying that will help them in turn if they take up the sport themselves. Rallying is one of those activities that you never learn unless you are there at the time. Being a service crewman is an excellent way of seeing people learn lessons the hard way – even if the people are their own driver or navigator!

Whereas it is the job of the driver to kit the service crew out with all the parts he will need, it is your job as navigator to ensure that the servicing arrangements actually work. This involves the inescapable duty of the navigator – thinking ahead. You must determine in your mind what you want your service crews to do. Sometimes, as on a road rally, they will simply be there to ensure that you have help in getting the car home if either it or your driver goes wrong. On the event itself they will probably hang around and watch you go by, and ensure that the trailer is taken safely from the start across to the finish. Sometimes you suspect that the car might need elaborate repairs and if a large supply of spare parts will be needed, you may need another chase car to visit points with a light load of emergency supplies, to enable your main service crew to travel slowly and safely to places where they can set up shop in ease. There is little point in taking equipment which you would never have to change. Sometimes you will have to worry about tyres which will need changing frequently, which may mean that you have less opportunity to carry large loads of spare equipment in addition. Each rally, indeed, each driver as well demands a different emphasis on the servicing, though it will be you who has to decide what emphasis the rally will demand. The main purpose of the servicing exercise

The ultimate in private rally service crews? This is the ''Birmingham Post'' team which supported John Bloxham and Richard Harper, on the 1974 Burmah Rally. Note the way that the crew are sitting patiently in the car, the axle stands placed under the car in case either crewman should jump out and upset the balance. The service vehicles (Range Rovers) are parked so that spares and tools can be reached easily.

so far as the navigator is concerned is to see that your men reach the points at which they will be of most use to you and your driver, although on events lower than International status the choice will rarely be yours — the organisers set up service areas that have to be adhered to and ban servicing elsewhere.

So, for Internationals, this raises two aspects: firstly at what points should they be situated, secondly how should they get there. The traditional point at which the crew should be placed is at every time control, where you may have time in hand whilst you wait to clock in, and after every special stage where the car will most likely need repair. This always seemed the most logical aim, and indeed this became the standard system for

servicing on British stage rallying for years. The notion of waiting at the end of stages came in for a rude shock the year that the Renault Alpines first arrived in Britain for the RAC Rally. They placed all their service points before the special stages! All of a sudden eyebrows were raised, and people realised that there was a lot more to planning service points than was obvious. Then when on an Italian rally tyre-changing service points were arranged in the middle of a stage, a chore became a science. Service crews can go anywhere that is not specifically forbidden, to help you as you need. The only difficulty for you is to decide what you will need, and when. Servicing can take forms other than actual attention to the car, it is a matter of win or crash on the Monte Carlo Rally for crews to know where the patches of ice can be expected on a test, it saves a lot of time for your aeroplane to fly above you on the Safari in East Africa and be told over the radio what spares you would like made ready at your next rendezvous point. All this activity is servicing in its style. But first things first, what are your priorities?

The first priority is for you to finish your rally. Therefore there is a mixed need for attention before a stage, to

A good example of an illuminated warning board on a pole. This is for you to spot where your service crew are stationed, even the other side of a bend . . .

ensure that a fault does not lead to complete failure when subjected to the strain of competition, and after a stage, to ensure that a part which broke on that stage is replaced and you can continue safely and without difficulty to the next stage. If a serious part has failed on a stage, it is unlikely that the car can be driven under its own power out of the stage, although it might be a part that can be simply replaced by the crew, and having a service vehicle ready at the finish might enable the car to be repaired and continue. Furthermore a service car waiting at the end of a stage will hear much sooner of trouble than one which left its post immediately the rally car started the stage — and made its

way to the next rendezvous. To have two crews, one at the start and one at the finish, would be nice, but two difficulties arise: you may only have one crew and if you stop twice between each stage you will soon fall badly behind schedule!

Beyond telling you of the sort of probelms you face in deciding where to place service crews, there is little more that can be said. You may well receive rules about where not to put crews. Sometimes you are told not to receive service on rally routes at certain stretches, often marked on a Tulip route card by a solid line. It is a question of interpretation of the individual regulations whether you can service in a lay-by off such a stretch of road. Usually it is implied that you can. You should have no trouble at all in servicing off the given route (there is usually no rule that you cannot leave rally route at a point and then regain it at the same point, unless the detour takes you into an area into which you are forbidden entry). Rules are different however when you are told you must not service until you reach a certain point. I cannot see any chance of beating such a rule, save that of making such a long detour off route that the chances of discovery are remote! Detours off route are time consuming, as you can imagine, for the distance off route is doubled by the competing car.

The other major task for you is marshalling the service crews so that they do not let you down. If a service crew misses a point, it will be your fault, barring mechanical misfortune of the service car. If the crew are not up to the schedule you planned, you should have assessed their limitation and planned an easier schedule instead. I have great feelings that only the most experienced service crews should be asked to stay up for more than one night. I well remember a couple of young fellows helping us mend our car where our own service crews were some way distant on one of the three-night Gulf Rallies. Later

Rough and ready methods often have to be used by service crews. Here a service car with a rope will straighten out a bent wing. A navigator has to be prepared to think of quick methods like this. This incident was on the 1971 Scottish.

Servicing is a job for those who are skilled at mechanical tasks but intelligent assistance by the navigator can always help. Here Terry Harryman holds a replacement driveshaft ready for Vic Elford's mechanic to fit. If in doubt, however, stay well clear.

Tony Mason leaves his Escort RS 1600 at a tyre changing point on the 1973 RAC Rally. A missed rendezvous can have serious consequences. Note the telephone box in the background, often salvation when plans are changed.

The bigger your class of rallying, the more people get involved but never get distracted! Jean-Marc Andrie beckons Jean Ragnotti into a control in Corsica at the correct moment.

that day they fell asleep at the wheel with fatal results. The three-night summer rallies like the Gulf were equivalent in tiredness to a two-night winter rally which is tough enough even for crews, who at least have the interest of the occasion to keep them going. Service crews do not have this stimulus. It is brave stuff asking your service crews to cover the maximum possible number of points but this leads to many bad things, their impatient driving, their lack of time to think of problems that you might need solving, quite apart from the likelihood of their missing a point. If the service crews make all their points it is a source of praise for them, but it is a tribute to your planning.

How to get them to their correct positions is the other aspect of your work. It is important to consider whether the service crew has a competent map-reader on board, and the size and agility of the vehicle concerned. I have quite a strong rule that service crews should never, save where absolutely essential, use by-roads. I would rather they were sited on the nearest main road and ask my driver to travel a further five miles

Service crews want to be part of the team. Few things give a service crew the chance of feeling quite so important as having to tow a broken competition car home. Normally a service car would not follow a competition car along the route − and never on a special stage − but if you expect an imminent failure, it is sensible to have them following behind. Here Tim Stock's Vauxhall Magnum is rescued from the M6 during the 1974 Tour of Britain.

along the rally route before we meet them than risk delay in having them travelling on minor roads. Not only are service cars a danger on minor roads, they cannot travel quickly along them, they are susceptible to police instruction to take a detour − and of course their crew might take the wrong road in the first place. There is enough congestion on minor roads near special stages with the influx of rally cars and spectators as it is.

Of necessity you will have to guess your service positions from the map. If you have been to a stage before you may well remember where it is possible to place your crews. Especially when there is guesswork it is important to arrange for your crew to have good warning boards. Once it was sufficient to have a warning board some distance in advance, but the easiness with which boards are forgotten in the rush to move on and the increasing number of service crews the present practice is to have a board upon a pole, illuminated for use at night, striking into the sky above your actual service van, so it can be seen from afar. At least such a board cannot be left behind − until the service car arrives at the first low bridge. In the appendix I have set out a typical schedule for a service crew, from which the instructions are self evident. On an International the crews will have Ordnance Survey maps, so that they will be able to find out how to back-

Servicing is now frowned upon on road rallies. Nigel Rockey and Clive Plummer are seen working on their Escort Twin cam a long time before servicing on club rallies came into vogue.

track along the route, and they will have a road book which gives references of the stages together with standard times. On a smaller rally the service point planning is more frantic. Sometimes the organisers prepare suggested (or even mandatory) instructions for service crews to follow, but these do not tell you everything. If you plot your route you often find that a prompt departure from the previous point and a clear run to the next point might enable the crew to see you as you pass that point earlier, on the way to the stage which the organisers had expected you to have to tackle before you receive service.

Chapter 13
Clever rallying

The use of brain power is the one factor that I cannot teach or explain within a book, because your brains are your own and you probably have ten times as many as me, anyway. You can obey all the instructions, your driver can be fastest on all the sections, but then some young imp beats you because he thought of something that had never occured to you at all. It pays to think of broader issues, to think of things from as many different angles as you can.

The first main decision you will have to make (hopefully!) is to decide which driver to go with. You may appear to have little choice, but most of us have only gone rallying because we have pestered drivers into taking us. Your choice is not so much which suitor to accept, rather which person to pester! You will have to become a master at judging people. The best person is often the poorest, for only a poor driver will try really hard to succeed whereas a rich one will not have the same hunger to succeed. The man with the fastest car is seldom the best choice, for to win overall you need the fastest driver rather than the fastest car, and a fast driver in a slow car will often have some class success

at least to gain. A fast driver in a slow car has everything to gain: a slow driver in a fast car has everything to lose! Never think of a driver as being the ultimate man in your life, for you can be certain that he will not consider you the ultimate man in his, unless you surprise each other during the rally with your respective abilities. If you amaze each other in this way, it will be because you do not know how much better still some other people are. Do not concern yourself too much with reputation of great danger, for such reputations are often built upon the stories of people who have no great knowledge of standards, and in any case one of your jobs is to manage a driver in such a way that he can be lured to the finish. What guidelines should you use to choose a driver? I think determination is the best guide.

Once you have chosen the right driver, your problems are only just beginning. I think a few examples of clever rallying might help to show what I mean!

At the Thornton le Dale time control on the 1971 RAC Rally there was an odd sight of Harry Kallstrom's Lancia Fulvia waiting outside the time control when all the cars around him were clocking in and making their way up the road. Thornton was an ordinary time control, not a halt where time lost had to be regained. It was coming on towards dusk on a winter's evening, and most early numbers would have made an urgent journey to the next special stages and tackle them before darkness fell. But Harry's navigator was not tempted. He stood fast and refused to clock in until he had used up every minute of the delay allowance he had accumulated at preceding stage starts. What was happening was this. Snow was lying in the hills and in these conditions an early number is anything but an advantage. The passage of cars clears much of the snow away, provides a better surface over which to drive — and gives faster times. Paul Faulkner on that rally was most unhappy to be seeded number 105 — yet this snow situation gave him an unexpected advantage and he came 15th overall. Harry's navigator played a gamble — that of not catching up on time when he could. The snow could have caused delays and he might have needed every minute he had spare, in order not to fall beyond maximum lateness at the next control. He correctly assessed the situation and stayed out of trouble. There was trouble in the hills however. A stage was cancelled and crews retired through baulking delays. Harry however was lucky. Clever rallying is seeing through general principles, looking at situations from a fresh point of view. All through the snowy sections on that rally, the leading crews were playing hide-and-seek, waiting up side turnings for as long as they dared, hoping that unsuspecting rivals would drive up to the starts of stages ahead of them.

There are a lot of things that a service crew do not know and you do, which in the heat of the moment you will not realise. Firstly, it is far from obvious in many cases which way the rally route will pass the service point. This is very worrying if you are an early runner, and your crew has to set up

their position before the rally arrives. Secondly, the business of when you are expected is less precise than you might think. So long as the service crew is given a shorter and simpler route than you will take from the last point, they will arrive ahead of you. This in turn makes life less easy for them. It is very nice for you to ask them to waste no time and arrive at the next point as soon as possible, but they will not know how long they have to wait once they get there. At night, it is nice for them to have a specific time when they know they are safe to be able to sleep in their van: it is not nice for you if you have sleepy service and irritable service crews or alternatively if you have to pull up, knock on their window and wait for them to rouse. Incidentally take good care to make sure you knock up the right people. We banged for ages waking up some luckless Datsun service crew on an RAC rally. Eventually even we reckoned that the faces were not familiar. They were servicing a Toyota that had not been expected for some quite long time.

Whatever you do, be nice to service crews. They are seldom being paid to keep you running, and want to be part of the team. To explain concisely what has been happening to you will give them an interest that keeps them going. If you are short with them, try to make it up to clear the air. Strains are easily created when you are tired and cold, and they stop a team working efficiently.

There are few absolutely golden rules for service cars, but one that has stood the test of time is never to leave a post unless the crew is given a written message from you to move. On innumerable occasions a crew has sensed that a rally car is in trouble and back-tracked down the route to find it. The vehicles have missed each other, the wounded car reaches the rendezvous point and the few precious minutes which were left for repairs are lost for ever. You should always carry some paper for giving messages in case you can't use a radio, and write out several. You cannot expect a car to stop on a stage for your message, so if you are stranded on a stage it may be essential for you to cut across to the end of the stage. Give out several of these messages to other competitors, for you can be sure if you give a message to only one car that car will break down itself, before it meets your service car! The design of a service van layout is an art, yet there are rarely two the same. Take a look inside factory team vans to pick up tips but always remember to fasten everything down well — a trolley jack flying around is not an aid to prolonged good health. Whatever your chosen service vehicle, it must be reliable — even more reliable than your rally car!

The final point about servicing is to establish by example a chain of command with the crew. If you take the initiative about their arrangements they know that what you say goes. Similarly make certain that the driver makes all the decisions about what is done on the car. He must decide how much petrol should be added, after you have advised about the distances and type of terrain to be covered. Even if navigating in itself leaves you feeling subservient, having control of the service crews gives you the obvious sense of authority you are lacking. But remember that hand-in-hand with pride of success goes responsibility for errors, and whatever they do wrong is basically down to you!

On the 1968 Targa Rusticana *Motoring News* Rally we had a strange example of finding it actually pays to elude the rules, sometimes. Like a chess player who sacrifices one piece for some greater prize later, it pays to think whether you will do better by some unorthodox manoeuvre. On the Targa there was lateness of thirty minutes, with a special penalty of 30 minutes' worth of penalty for every minute early on the petrol-halt sections, as against the usual minute penalty for lateness. At the second petrol halt the future pattern of the rally was clear. It would be mighty hard to avoid running into 'fails', that is falling beyond maximum lateness, yet with the 30-minute penalty at the control after the second halt there was frustration at being unable to get on with the rally. Then Rod and Ian Cooper realised that the penalty for early arrival, huge though it was, was nothing compared with the alternatives, so they went into the control 13 minutes early. Only two other crews avoided the fails that night, so with their extra 390 minute penalty Rod and Ian came third. The 30-minute penalty was intended to stop any such thing, to stop people hurrying through the built up areas, to give ample time for everyone to fill up with petrol — and not give leading crews unobstructed by queues an advantage. But you play the ball where it lies. You can rely on the rules and base your tactics accordingly.

Some rules are wrong. There was a bad case in a Scottish rally where the maximum penalty was wrongly set by a factor of ten so that on a stage of any length one would inevitably incur that maximum. Crews who spotted this cruised through without risking car or causing unnecessary wear and tear to no avail. The rule was changed later in the event but no rules can be changed retrospectively. Sometimes times are wrongly set. On the 1970 RAC the nine-mile stage at Blackcraig in Scotland was given a six-minute bogey time, which in the icy conditions was impossible even for the Finns! On a club event you cannot rely on the accuracy of watches and must accept what they say, but on an International you can. Anyone who spotted this error knew that the watches could not be fiddled to overcome the error, and did not try to go quickly. Only a handful completed the test within the maximum penalty.

Sometimes it pays to hold yourself back and not correct what you know to be wrong. On the Chieftain which we spoke about earlier, we were all given a penalty in excess of the maximum. On studying the times of our rivals, we found their times were greater than ours. It was up to them to complain, not us. There is no obligation to draw the attention of an organiser to one of his errors, any more than if a marshal *gives* you a minute. Sportsmanship only dictates that you do not complain when the error is discovered! It never pays to tell the world too much of your troubles, particularly if they are serious. Jokes about the minor ones, by all means! The organisers may forget about the road penalties on a stage event, your rival may hear you have an ailing car and press you especially hard rather than cruising to a secure position behind you.

Every navigator makes mistakes. Even Stuart Turner expected his navigators to err every two or three years! The best navigator is the one who spots the error the quickest. This may be a matter of spotting that the map is wrong on a road event, it might be noticing that you have overshot the junction you wanted. Sometimes it is a matter of spotting an organiser's mistake. David Stephenson did not hesitate on the 1970 Cilwendeg when he realised that a control was in the wrong place, and this enabled him to cut out a large portion of the route. He kept his secret until the results were finalised, though.

To what extent is it sporting to abuse the weakness of the organisation? Without entering this realm too far, I think we can best think of rallying as a sport and do what others do. If you would not wish to boast of what you did, when all is over, then you have overstepped the mark. If you do things which will turn organisers away from the thought of providing you with your sport, then you have gone too far. This is so much a personal thing.

There was once a person on the *Motoring News* rounds (not me!) who always tried to steal a march on the marshals by leaving controls early in the late sections of a rally. If this was done on an earlier section there was always the chance that he would be reported and a penalty imposed. On the later stages, however, this was less likely, for immediately a competitor arrived at the finish of the rally the roadbooks would be marked so the marshal would not have had time to inform the organisers. Anyway a late section marshal would quite likely not go to the end. Winning is always the name of the game, but then so is personal satisfaction. If this satisfies, well and good. Conscience in many ways depends upon what is expected. If your rivals will be doing just as you are doing, there is no deception.

Rallymanship comes in many forms. What should you say to your driver when you get frightened? Every navigator in the book starts to tell his driver that the corners are just a little sharper than they are or that the corner is just a little nearer than it really is. With good drivers, good navigators do not get frightened. You both want to win. Do not let this desire get the better of you, although it is a temptation to tell your driver, when you have a puncture, that it is only a mile to the control when it is two, it is silly to exaggerate. Let him take the blame for a wrong decision. If the wheel collapses and the suspension breaks in consequence, do not ever let it be your fault. The truth will always come out. Your driver's eye will be glued to your service car's tripmeter when you drive back down the stage to collect the remains of your car! If you start lying to your driver about the sharpness or the distance the corner is away, any faith he had in you will have gone. He will drive entirely upon his own judgement and you will be more terrified than ever. If you think he is going faster than is sensible, say so. My only suggestion is that you wait just a corner or two, in case your driver really is a wonder boy!

Quite an equally important aspect of rallymanship is how you get on with your driver in the car. It is difficult to change your character, and nothing is less worthy than a forced character.

This does not stop you trying to develop a manner which encourages and gratifies a driver. Drivers are, almost to a man, vain creatures who love signing autographs and seeing their names at the head of the stage times, and it is unhelpful if you try to do anything in public to detract from the impression your driver hopes to give.

Always let your driver talk to the Press, it's him they are interested in after all — but always brief him to say the right thing first! Speak about these matters, should they worry you, by all means but only in private. But more than tact, the proper basis for a successful partnership is a businesslike one. Almost as many friendships are lost through rallying as are created, and every failure is the result of thoughtlessness and lack of business sense.

Money is the centre of practically every dispute, so before you ever go rallying be absolutely sure what it will cost you. Let us take a small club event to begin with. You have the cost of petrol, insurance and entry fee staring at you large. These things are easily assessed in advance, so make it be clear between you in what proportions they are to be paid — and when they are to be paid. Make certain that other risks fall on the driver. Make certain, furthermore, that you pay for the things like maps and navigational equipment, that are more use to you afterwards. Every bent wing, every ruined tyre must be his problem. Remember that three-quarters of the glory goes to him, only the other quarter to you. Remember also that the driver must always carry the can ultimately, and if you make a mistake it was his fault for taking you! In exchange for this arrangement he takes pick of the prizes. If there are cups or awards specially for the navigator then those, and only those, are yours. Let us take for a further example an International event. Never on your life agree to split all the costs. It might sound silly, but I have seen it

done, and I have seen friends fall out over it in consequence. A driver owns his car, and any work in preparation on the car adds to its value. None of that expense is down to you. Any bonuses that come your way, either from the organisers or from the trade, are down to him. Next time he will surely lose the lot. Never make arrangements over and above what you can afford. There will always be expenses which you never anticipated. Never be shy of putting an arrangement down in writing — in a letter is best of all. This will not frighten off any driver you would want to go with, and can only impress him with attention to detail. If the driver is the sort of person who might be offended by this sort of approach, then it is probably better to have the misunderstanding before an event, for surely rallying with a person who is casual over this sort of aspect will only lead to bitterness afterwards. Make sure you settle up with your driver as soon after the event as possible, before you spend money that is owing to him, and before each of you begins to forget expenses you have incurred which should be brought into account.

Is it better to form a regular partnership or to freelance from driver to driver? I have always enjoyed going with as many different drivers as I can. It is amazing what a range of occupations you find in rallying. A lot of people are in the motor trade, but I can claim solicitors, licensed slaughterers, panel beaters and countless others. Every one has a different style of life. I think it is fun seeing how other people live and think. There is no class distinction. I enjoy the closeness to the sport that service crews enjoy, something that is missing in other, similar sports. If you are entering a championship of rallies there is every advantage in teaming up with a particular driver. You will need money and nobody is interested in supporting a one-off effort on a relatively minor event. You will have the opportunity of streamlining your administration, you will be able to rely (or be warned you cannot rely!) on the other person carrying out some function. This will enable you in particular to have time on concentrating on the finer points of preparing for the event, which is good. Choosing a partner for a year demands skill. Do you know the person well enough to know he will keep his enthusiasm? Do you know that he will not run out of money half way through a season? Think a long while before making a decision, and never be afraid to ask common friends for their confidential opinions. The number of times you hear people saying 'If only you had asked me, I could have told you he had two wives/had been made bankrupt/had funny habits/always mislaid his competition licence'. Once again, the only person who would object to your asking for a second opinion is the person who has a problem to hide. It is an exercise in judging people, something that is all part of the fun of rallying.

If you form a partnership, make it clear at the outset not only the respective financial arrangements but the limits to the partnership. Times without number I hear stories like 'and of course he has gone and navigated so and so, who has a better car than mine. I know it was outside our original agreement but I would have thought he would have asked me first'. His fault for assuming things, but lack of foresight on your part for not making intentions clear in the first place. You often get better known as a navigator if you stick to one person ('Oh he is the person who is always getting that fellow lost' — all publicity is good publicity!) which must be a good thing until you have a few results under your belt and you can stand on your own merits.

How much should you contribute to a driver? This is the inevitable business thing. You measure how much you want to rally with the person concerned against how much he needs you. Knowing yourself is an immensely valuable asset. If you know you can be relied upon to get good results, when drivers and cars permit, then you can expect to be taken on rallies for nothing. Against this you must bear in mind how much your sport would suffer if you were denied the chance of getting those results — either because you priced yourself out of the market or because your attitude only provided you with rides in uncompetitive cars. Knowing what people think of you is another asset. If you can impress your driver with your competence, not only does it help on the event but the driver goes home and tells his mates. It might be your persuasive ability of getting a good starting number, it might be your way of convincing a marshal that a minute is neither here nor there so far as he is concerned, it might be the way you persuade the manager of an overbooked hotel that he has a room for you and your driver. Remember you have expenses of your own to defray come what may, the maps being a really costly item these days, in particular if you agree to share certain expenses, only share those expenses which will be readily assessible in advance, and will not prove an undue burden if you have to retire early. Petrol is an expense that is proportional to the distance you travel, unless you hole the petrol tank and leave twenty gallons evaporating in the road. Bear also in mind just how much petrol a competition car will use. Eight to ten miles a gallon is nothing unusual when the car is driven in anger. Remember also that you use much less petrol when there are long liaison sections, or on fast rallies where much of the running is in a high gear.

How much should you force your will on a driver? I always feel that you should hold your opinions back as far as possible. Your job is to inform a driver of the facts and leave him to make his decisions. Even if a driver is driving wildly I always try to contain my anxiety, perhaps a little too much as my accident record shows! It is always difficult for you to know whether the sudden skids are a symptom of dangerous driving or just his style. Perhaps I let my hate of coming second overrule my head, but I always dread the day when I restrain a driver to the extent that we lose. You are not really qualified to tell a driver how to drive, any more than he is to tell you how to navigate. Having said this never be too proud to let him tell you little ideas that other navigators have, and in turn with an emphasis on the 'interesting little item of information' you might say how you once worked out how much time could be saved by taking smoother lines through corners, or telling the joke about the bloke who crashed the very last corner and had to carry the pieces of car over the finishing line, only to be disqualified because he left his navigator behind in the bushes. If that doesn't work, then write the driver off as someone who finds it hard to learn! Accidents are very frustrating for a navigator, but they are part of the sport. There are two ways a driver reaches the height of his sport. One is the boring way of gradually getting quicker. The other is the exciting way of being naturally quick and only slowly getting safer!

Chapter 14
Getting yourself organised

If you think of yourself as the rally manager, the person who makes certain everything goes right and who leaves the driver to do his thing without any unnecessary care, you will have to accept that there is a lot of detailed work in your job. This is only an effort when it cannot be dealt with smoothly. When you have yourself organised it is a pleasure to see things being dealt with when other people are failing to get entries or are being given poor starting numbers simply because they were not organised.

Rallying these days is quite as much a publicity exercise as a sport. Some people are wealthy enough to regard it entirely as a sport. Fair enough, but never let me hear you complain about the expense of rallying or that you were beaten simply because the other fellow had a more expensive car! But whoever we are we will still have to sell ourselves, in particular to the organisers, if we wish to have our entry accepted and be given a good starting number. And if we are in the position of hoping that someone with a fairy bag of gold will come our way, the time to start regarding the sport as a publicity exercise is now, before we have any

added commercial responsibilities on our shoulders. Show people that you can help yourself, and then others will be inclined to help you in turn. How do we sell ourselves? Let's think about the simple business of entering a rally, for example.

We saw earlier that we have to obtain copies of the regulations of the event we wish to enter, through our club bulletin or maybe advertisement in the motoring weeklies. Sometimes if we are on the mailing list of our club or an area association we will have regulations sent to us automatically. We read the regulations, find our driver and decide to enter. The basic thing you need in order to enter, apart from a competition licence and club membership, is the entry form and cheque for the fee. Now, put yourself in the place of the person who is entry secretary of the event you wish to enter. You receive sometimes hundreds of entry forms and cheques, some legible and some not so, and your entry form and cheque will hardly mark you down as someone special. You may find favour in being notably more legible than the others, but that is hardly likely to make you eligible for the special favours you would like. But

In the days before commercial interests took a hold on rallying there used to be many more manufacturers interested in the sport, which meant many more professional opportunities to competitors. This is Bobby Parkes in a works Reliant Sabre 6 in 1963.

wait, why do we want the favours? What can or should an organiser do for us, more than anyone else? One always hopes that should our entry arrive the day that the lists fill up then it is our entry that is chosen rather than the others. Wishful thinking, perhaps, but surely a fairer thing to hope for is a good starting number. We have seen earlier that a low number is not always a good thing, as in snowy conditions or where grassy stages dry out during the passage of cars, but a low number helps enormously with publicity. The tired old press photographer that the local paper sends down to the start will not wait till number 95 reaches the starting ramp. He will long since have gone home. So, how do we get a number that befits our self-importance?

Number one essential in any entry form is to make certain the organisers know your competition record. Over-elaboration of excuses only bores, over-detail simply confuses, but a neat list of previous results will show your true worth and tell the organisers that you care. Never lie on your form. Do not put too many irrelevant items down. When I have formed a rally partnership we have produced a little sheet showing the successes of driver and navigator which can be slipped in with the entry form. Practically every entry form nowadays has a separate space for previous results to be listed. Let the organisers have your list even if they do not ask for details. Organisers never like being hounded in the days before a start by competitors who want a number changed. This only leads to broken promises or rude rebuffs. If you know a person ahead of you is not starting, see if you can swop with him and tell the organisers that he agrees. The organisers may still be unwilling. They may already have prepared a neat results board with everyone's name on it, and they may genuinely be put out of joint to have an unnecessary change.

What other than a good number can we achieve? The goodwill of the

". . . faceless people following the results, watching rallies and reading reports . . ." Stuart Turner, Public Relations Director of the Ford Motor Company watches the Rally of the Plains.

organisers! Any organiser worth his salt will have interested the local press, and the inevitgable question that a local pressman will ask is for the names of the interesting competitors. Maybe he will simply wish to list them down like prizewinners in the village produce show, but equally he might like to run a story on a particular hero who aims to win. Further, enthusiastic organisers will run a programme for the spectators. If organisers cater for spectators they can channel them away from areas where they would cause a nuisance, and there is nothing like a programme for this purpose. Your picture in a rally programme is really something! So how do you achieve such an honour? There is never any guaranteed success. Nothing in advertising, whether commercial or personal, is ever

guaranteed, but success comes when you least expect it. If you cover the available opportunities, success will follow. When you send in your entry form, why not enclose an action picture of you and your driver as well? Most events have photographers who will sell pictures to you afterwards, and if you order in quantity you will usually obtain a decent discount. We have often sent organisers mug-shots of ourselves as well, not because I or most of my drivers could ever be said to be pretty, but because it helps to create in the mind of the organiser the impression that we are serious. When you are a poor voluntary worker helping your friend run his rally and you have twenty people clamouring for your attention at the same time, you will tend to speak first to the person you know, or think you know. Basic psychology. The number of times I have ever obtained direct benefit from being known is small, but the times I have had indirect benefit are without number. Try it and see. It is well worth the cost of a few pictures. It may be of no help to you at all, but then suddenly you may find your action picture is used on the front of the regulations for next year's event.

If and when you reach the level of being sponsored, you have obligations to fulfil in this field. Sponsorship is a two-way business. It is never a gratuity. If a person gives you money or parts for you to use on your car, you offer in return your time as well as the space on your car. You must take time to think of ways of promoting the affairs of your sponsor. When we enter rallies we always include photographs of the car, preferably in action, which show the sponsor's name to best advantage. We spend hours looking at pictures of the car to see just how best the stickers can show up. Brooklyn Garages produced some really striking stickers for their customers and for Russell Brookes that looked lovely, until the pictures came out. The colours on the stickers were such that one merged into the other and hardly any picture of Russell in action could show the words. It was only when the windscreen stickers began to be used

did Brooklyn begin to get any real publicity mileage out of pictures used in magazines. The Goodyear stickers, great bold things with black letters on a white background have always stood out well. Then spend time looking at rally car pictures in magazines and see where on the car the stickers should be placed if they are to be read. People place stickers firmly on bonnets, oblivious of the way that a camera will never pick out the words at a shallow angle. Until the windscreen stickers came along, the registration number plate was always easily the best read sticker on the car! You as navigator have time to think about these things, your driver with oily hands every night has not. Even consider the colour of your car. A dark coloured car on a night time road rally looks indiscernable from the background in a flash photo — light coloured cars are the only ones seen in the motoring weeklies.

What else can you do to reward a sponsor? We have seldom become involved in the sticker war, fortunately,

Sponsors can come from every imaginable source. What better than Camel cigarettes who supply attractive ladies to aid their publicity.

Jon Cleary's Ford Escort RS 2000 sponsored by T. W. Robinson's — a demolition company.

but we always obtained brochures from sponsors to give to rally organisers so that they can see to whom we owe our allegiances — and more than that, can see that we are being serious in what we do. Involvement with a magazine is nice, for every now and again we can arrange for copies to be given to the marshals, and this makes our arrival all the more interesting for them.

Keeping track of things is pretty essential. A calendar is vital to save clashes of arrangements. One person who in the early seventies was heavily involved in rally sponsorship entered three events one night with the same car. The RAC MSA gets hopping mad at this sort of thing, for it messes organisers up no end — particularly in speed events where organisers advertise who will take part — but this fellow had a most persuasive manner and eventually explained how it was all a big mistake. Make certain you don't have to talk yourself out of trouble. Get

things right, do not put them right. A file for individual events helps things immensely. It means that next year you can refer to your file and remember the things you could have done but forgot, the people you would do well to contact, the things that were unusual and almost caught you out. If you are in a championship things can get quite hectic when there is a run of events on consecutive week-ends. You enter an event six weeks hence, you chase up an entry for which you have not had acknowledgement four weeks hence, you query the rules of an event two weeks hence, you swot up the rules for this week's event and you arrange the date for a protest of an event that happened two weeks ago!

All this work sounds like a lot of effort that you could do without, and so it is, but it is the thing that makes you useful to a driver and consistent winning never came easy. Even harder work is negotiating with people to help you finance your rallying. Some drivers, particularly the professional ones, regard this as their province exclusively — a sort of professional jealousy which is understandable. Any navigator will invariably have had more experience at setting up schemes than an amateur driver, and this is one of the spheres where your advice is invaluable. There is a basic principle to consider when making plans, that is to remember that any sponsorship is the two-way arrangement. It is a sort of employment, a sort of sale of publicity facility. If you fail to do the job or fail to produce the effort which publicity demands you have failed your sponsor, erased your name from his books for evermore, and maybe even disillusioned that sponsor altogether with the sport.

It is always difficult to know just what companies or agencies expect to get out of rallying, but before you do a deal — be it for £10 or £10,000, you are doomed to disaster unless you try to find out. The usual reasons are these: promoting a product before a large number of people, producing a product which a company will want a winning crew to use, having a focal point in an exciting activity which will characterise a company's image and lastly giving a business person the opportunity to be involved in something exciting that time or opportunity forbids him to do personally. Each of these reasons demands different approaches. Each of them is only attractive to a certain type of driver or rally team. Each of them demands a different sort of feedback and level of behaviour. And if you fail to understand the purpose, you might as well not take the venture on for all the ultimate good it will do you or the sport.

The next thing to bear in mind is that money is not the only form of sponsorship you can get. Supply of parts and supply of labour are quite as valuable. Much of sponsorship is some form of fiddle! It might be the fiddle of offering something which costs a company a lot less than its worth to you. It might be the fiddle of tax allowances, it might be the fiddle of parting with unsaleable stock! There are sometimes things more useful than

money. Work out what you want. You might have a local printing business interested in supporting you. Make certain that you get all the nicely printed notepaper you would ever need as well as money! You might have an oil company interested in helping you. Think of the various problems your driver could be having and do not fight shy of asking for advice, or even enquiring if you could have equipment analysed. A lot of sponsoring companies want to be used. They often go in for sponsoring as a way of getting involved and finding out if there is a future in further involvement in the sport.

You are the brains of the outfit. Your driver takes you on rallies not just because you amuse him or you contribute something material to the exercise. he takes you so that he can relieve himself of all the worry about things which do not particularly concern him — or do concern him but he does not know how to handle. Eventually you may start finding that rallying begins to pay for itself, and is no longer the expensive luxury that once it was. As soon as this happens you can justify time and effort to a greater degree and can keep on rallying without worrying about the effect it has on other aspects of your life. As soon as you reach this level, your degree of usefulness becomes even greater. The more years you stay in the sport the more people you meet, the more lessons you learn. It is for this reason that there are very few young navigators earning a living out of the sport.

Financially rewarding rallying starts generally at the Dealer Team level. Up to this level you will hope you do not lose on your sport, but inevitably you will be losing in terms of not earning good money at some other pursuit. At this level you are unlikely to earn a fee but you should receive day money, a lump sum for every day you spend away from home to cover hotels and meals, with any invoicable item for fares, petrol necessarily incurred on your duties being payable separately. This sum will cover your needs and give you an incentive to lead a frugal existence, though such intentions will usually dissipate at the bar when the work is done. The chance of earning a fee at rallying is always fairly remote, and for obvious reasons only those who do not have a prior responsibility to employers can expect regular work. Even that depends on the law of supply and demand!

You can be sure of one thing, that even as an impoverished clubman there will be faceless people following the results, watching rallies and reading the reports. They are thinking about the future. The future may bring them no opportunities for sporting participation or it may. Whatever the future holds they are watching and thinking who it would be nice for them to have in their rally team, if they are allowed to have one. Few things help them in their dreaming more than a string of good results but there will be more than results when the final decisions are made. They want people capable of being in command of their rally cars, their drivers and themselves, and I hope this book has given a few ideas on how you can accomplish this objective. I hope, also, that it will give you the chance of enjoying every minute of your rally sport, to whatever level you aspire.

APPENDIX 1
How to plot a map reference

Every 50,000 Series map is divided into kilometre squares with reference numbers based upon an imaginary point off the south-west corner of the country. The vertical lines up and down the map are numbered along the top and bottom of the map, and these numbers represent the distance east from that imaginary point. The horizontal lines which are numbered up and down each side represent the distance north of the point. Map references are given by reference firstly to the Easting distance and then the Northing distance. For the purpose of map references on rallies the number of the map is usually given first, and consequently the number of hundreds of kilometres can be omitted as superfluous.

An imaginary six-figure map reference can be given as follows: 123/456789. This refers firstly to map number 123. Next we must find the relevant kilometre square on the map. Look firstly at the Eastings, and find '45' and then at the Northings and find '78'. Then in the square concerned use the romer to measure the point 6/10ths across the square and 9/10ths up the square. This gives you the reference to the nearest 100 metres. Eight figure references can be either by adding fractions, thus 123/456½789¾, which

can easily be interpreted by the romer, or by decimals, thus 123/45657897, which is equivalent to our other example.

Tips on map reading

Always work from the map to the road, in other words find the feature on the map and then tell the driver to look for it. Only when lost should you look to find the feature on the roadside and then try to find it on the map!

Remember that roads are shown on maps as though they were sixty or seventy yards wide, whereas they are much narrower in fact. Thus many corners are shown as generalisations. If you approach a corner that looks like a 45 degrees right and the road indicates it goes first to the left, be warned that the actual right-hander will be that much sharper when you reach it.

It is easiest to navigate by turning the map round so you are always reading 'uphill'. In this way you will seldom confuse your left with your right, as you will always be reading the map the way you will see the road.

It is less tiring on the head muscles and the eyes if you hold your map up rather than down.

APPENDIX 2
RAC Competition Licences

The application form for Competition Licences (form 8301) and explanatory notes (form 8388) are available from: **The RAC Motor Sports Association Ltd., 31 Belgrave Square, London SW1X 8QH.**

The following pages of Appendix 2 show reproductions of both these forms as well as a specimen Competition Licence.

RAC MSA COMPETITION LICENCE

ISSUED BY THE RAC MOTOR SPORTS ASSOCIATION LTD
31, BELGRAVE SQUARE,
LONDON SW1X 8QH ENGLAND

DRIVER/CONDUCTEUR   LICENCE NUMBER

ENTRANT/CONCURRENT

Holders signature ....
Date of Birth (if under 21)...

RAC

1983

Only valid if
Photograph of
Holder is
affixed here
and licence
is signed

This licence is valid for:-

EXPIRES DECEMBER 31st 1983

SAMPLE

RAC
Motor Sports Association Ltd.
COMPETITION LICENCES AND ADVERTISING PERMITS
TERMS OF ISSUE 1983
FORM 8388

YOUR COMPETITION LICENCE

1.1. A Competition Licence, issued by The RAC Motor Sports Association Ltd, is required for most forms of Motor Sport organised under a Permit issued by the MSA.

Licences are available for:
  Race
  Rally
  Speed Events (excluding Racing)
  Kart
  Trade Entrant
  Rally Navigator
  Temporary (not Racing)
In addition two licences cater for the Club enthusiast:
  'Clubman C' – Valid for Restricted and National Autotest, Trial and 4 W.D.
  'Clubman RS' – Valid as Clubman C plus Restricted Rallies and Closed, or Restricted, Speed events (excluding Racing).

1.2. Applicants for all licences use application form No. 8301. The type and grade of licence valid for various events is shown in table on page 6.

1.3. Foreign Nationals must obtain a letter of Authorisation from the governing body of motor sport in their own country before the MSA can issue a Competition Licence.

1.4. National and International Grade Licences (other than Speed) are only available after observation at Closed or Restricted events. (See Upgrading Procedure 5.)

1.5. Competitors who do not hold an RTA Licence and/or who are under 18 (see 10) may participate in Grass Track, 2CV Cross, Mini Cross, Production or Sporting Trials and Autotests. They should take out a Clubman RS or Clubman C as appropriate for these events. Non-driving Navigators should take out a Navigator's R or N Licence.

1.6. A temporary Non-racing Licence is available for 14 days for certain events only.

GRADES OF EVENT AND LICENCE

2.1. Car Events are classified in six grades in ascending order:
Closed: Open only to members of the organising club.
Co-Promoted: Open to members of the co-promoting clubs only.
Restricted: Open only to members of clubs listed in the regulations of the event.
National: Open to any qualified competitor licensed by the MSA but not to holders of foreign licences.
International: Open to all qualified competitors of any nationality so long as FIA rules allow them to take part (FIA rules restrict certain successful drivers to Full International events outside their own country).
International Open (or Full International): Open to all qualified competitors of any nationality holding a licence issued with the authority of the FIA.

2.2. All drivers' licences also permit the holder to act as an entrant for himself.

2.3. The co-driver or navigator in a rally of Restricted or higher status requires a Driver's Competition Licence. For anyone unable or not intending to drive there is the Navigator's Licence. This licence is not valid as an entrant, or for International events.

2.4. International Race Licences are subdivided into 'A', 'B' and 'C'.

2.5. An International Racing 'A' Licence is valid for Formula One Events (other than the World Championship for Drivers), USAC Championship events plus events covered by International 'B' or 'C' Licences. An International Racing 'B' Licence is valid for F2, F3, F Atlantic, F5000, Can-Am, Group 5 and 6 of 3 litres or over. An International 'C' Licence is valid for all other International Car Races.

2.6. KART COMPETITION LICENCES are available for either Kart Circuits only (Short Circuit

Licences) or for both Kart Circuits and Long Circuits (a Long Circuit is a recognised Motor Racing Circuit or a track exceeding 1500m in length).

2.6.1. Short Circuit Licences are divided into two grades – Novice and International. A driver is classed as a Novice until he has completed 4 events satisfactorily. An International S/C licence is also valid as a NOVICE for long ciruits.

2.6.2. Short Circuit Licences are also available for Juniors aged 11 upwards.

2.6.3. The full Kart Licence, which is valid for both Long and Short circuits, is also split into two grades – Novice and International with similar up-grading requirements.

2.6.4. A Medical Certificate is required if competing in Long Circuit Kart events.

2.7. ENTRANT. If it is desired to have an entry at a car or Kart event, in the name of an organisation, firm or sponsor, or person who will not drive, an ENTRANT'S LICENCE must be obtained.

Official programmes and results must state the title or name of an entrant and/or driver exactly as it is stated on the appropriate competition licence. The maximum number of words permitted in an Entrant's title is six.

2.7.1. RAC Recognised clubs may apply for an Entrant's Licence and 5 copies free of charge.

ADVERTISING

3.1. A DRIVER'S and/or ENTRANT'S Licence (or Waiver K 1.8) permits a limited amount of advertising to be shown on either or both sides of the car, but not facing forward or rearward. The limit is:

3.1.1. The Name of Entrant, once on each side of the car in letters not exceeding 4½in high.

3.1.2. The Name of the Driver, once on each side of the car in letters not exceeding 4in high.

3.1.3. The Make of the Car (or name of Mechanic) once on each side of the car in letters not exceeding 3½in high.

3.1.4. A maximum of 5 decals, not exceeding 55sq.in each, on each side of the car. These decals may not be on the front or back, and may not be related to form a name or message.

3.1.5. The competitor must make available to the organiser an area of 100sq.in on each side of the car, adjacent to the space allocated for showing the vehicle's competition number, and clearly visible, on which the organiser may specify the event, its sponsor or the course on which it is being run.

3.1.6. The competitor taking part in an event of a championship series must make available an area of 100sq.in on each side of the car on which the organiser may specify the championship and its sponsor (if that sponsor is different from the sponsor of the individual event) so long as the competitor is required to display only the title of the championship.

3.1.7. No display may contain offensive material.

3.1.8. All displays to be made by the competitor must be specified in the application for entry to the event and must be in place when the vehicle is scrutineered.

3.1.9. No display interferes with easy identification of the vehicle's competition number.

3.2. If additional advertising is required (except for the name of the car in Drag Racing), an ADVERTISING PERMIT must be purchased for each car. This permit allows unlimited advertising, subject to certain provisos, and is available in three grades – Restricted, National, International. Competitors must carry the appropriate Permit for the grade of event in which they are competing.

3.2.1. An Advertising Permit is NOT an Entrant's Licence.

3.3. Advertising Permits can only be obtained by Competition Licence holders.

3.3.1. A permit relates to one specific vehicle only and the permit, a self-destruct sticker, must be fixed in an easily visible place on the vehicle instrument panel.

3.3.2. If it is decided to transfer a permit from one vehicle to another the sticker must be removed and its remains returned to the MSA with a stamped addressed envelope and a request for a free issue of a replacement sticker.

3.4. An Advertising Permit authorises unrestricted publicity to be shown on a car, subject to 3.1.5.–3.1.9. and the following:

3.4.1. The authorisation may be withdrawn or modified by the organiser of an event if it is to be televised or is an event for historic cars, so long as the organiser obtains the prior approval of the MSA and gives not less than one month's written notice to the competitor or specifies any such restriction in the Supplementary Regulations.

3.4.2. No display placed on a transparent surface is more than 5in deep.

MEDICAL CERTIFICATES

4.1. Drivers in Circuit Races require a valid current Medical Certificate. The blank form is supplied automatically with all RACE Licences. A driver competing in an International Race MUST have his medical certificate endorsed by a medical practitioner appointed by the MSA prior to the event. The fee for endorsement is included in the Licence Fee. 21 days must be allowed for processing.

4.2. Drivers must agree to their medical attendant providing any relevant information which may be required by any medical practitioner acting for the MSA.

UPGRADING PROCEDURE

5.1. For a driver to obtain a Race, Rally or Kart Competition Licence of a grade higher than Restricted, he or she must already be qualified to hold such a licence or qualify in accordance with the criteria below.

5.2. A request for upgrading signature has to be made to the organisers, and if the results of the event show that the driver's performance was satisfactory, his Competition Licence will be signed in the space provided. In the case of races and Kart races only the MSA Steward of the Meeting is empowered to sign -- for rallies the Clerk of the Course signs. Qualification must be obtained in chronological order within the preceding 24 months.

The requisite qualifications for upgrading are:

Racing

5.3.1. RESTRICTED TO NATIONAL. Receive Steward's signatures in six Restricted or Closed races. These must not all be at the same circuit.

5.3.2. NATIONAL TO INTERNATIONAL 'C'. Hold a National Licence and receive Steward's signatures in two National or one National plus two Restricted, or five Restricted races. Again not all on the same circuit.

5.3.3. INTERNATIONAL 'C' TO INTERNATIONAL 'B'. Hold a Grade 'C' International Licence and finish among the first five in five International races within a period of 12 months, or have held a National or International 'C' Licence for at least one calendar year, and have finished in the first five in at least ten International/National/Restricted Championship events for either single seat or sports racing cars on at least 3 different circuits within a period of 24 months.

5.3.4. INTERNATIONAL 'B' TO INTERNATIONAL 'A'. Hold a Grade 'B' International Licence and finish among the first five in five International races for single seat cars of at least F2 status within a period of 12 months prior to application, or finish among the first five in ten International Open Formula 3 or Formula Atlantic races, or their British Championship equivalent, within a period of 24 months prior to application.

5.3.5. Historic car events do not qualify for upgrading to either International 'B' or International 'A' Licences.

5.3.6. HISTORIC INTERNATIONAL GRADE. Finish in four races for Historic Cars.

Rallies

5.4.1. RESTRICTED TO NATIONAL. Finish in four rallies of which at least one must be of Restricted grade.

5.4.2. NATIONAL TO INTERNATIONAL. Qualify for a National Licence and finish in one National or two Restricted rallies.

5.4.3. Rally Navigators should upgrade their licences from Restricted to National as in 5.4.1

above. Rally Navigators who are also Co-Drivers can upgrade from National to International Rally Driver as in 5.4.2 above.

Speed

5.5.1. No specific qualification is required for upgrading a Speed Licence.

Kart

5.6.1. NOVICE S/C TO INTERNATIONAL S/C. Obtain Steward's signature at 4 events.

5.6.2. NOVICE KART TO INTERNATIONAL KART. Obtain Steward's signature at 6 events, two of which must have been long circuit events.

DOWNGRADING

6.1. A 1983 National or International Licence for Race, Rally or Kart will only be issued to an applicant who has either:

(a) Held such a Licence during 1980, 1981 or 1982.

or

(b) Qualified for upgrading as detailed in Section 5.

6.1.1. Competitors who held an International Race or Rally Licence during 1978 or 1979 will be entitled to apply for the appropriate National Licence.

6.1.2. All other applicants will only be entitled to apply for a Restricted Licence.

6.2. To maintain an International 'A' or International 'B' Licence the driver must participate in at least one International race (other than Historic) per 12 month period, otherwise the driver will revert to an International 'C' Licence.

FOREIGN EVENTS

7.1. A competition licence holder proposing to compete in an event outside the United Kingdom is required by FISA Rules to first obtain the MSAs permission. If this permission is granted a 'visa' document will be issued.

7.2. For drivers the 'visa' includes insurance in respect of medical expenses up to a maximum of £2,500.

PERIOD OF VALIDITY

8.1. Unless otherwise rendered invalid, all 1983 licences and advertising permits run from the date of issue and for a maximum period of 13 months, from 1st December 1982 to 31st December 1983.

INSPECTION OF LICENCES AND ADVERTISING PERMITS

9.1. Licences and Permits must be produced for inspection at all events prior to a competitor taking part therein. Failure to produce a correct and valid licence may lead to exclusion.

9.1.1. If the Stewards of a Meeting – and only the Stewards may do this – waive this penalty they must charge the competitor a non-

3

refundable fee which shall be not less than the appropriate licence fee.

9.1.2. It follows that a competitor cannot be allowed to start if there is any question of his right to the correct grade of licence for the event.

9.2. Only the originals of licences and permits are acceptable. Photocopies are not acceptable.

9.2.1. One Entrant's Licence covers all the entries at a meeting in the name of that Entrant.

9.3. Non-production of an advertising permit, where the displays on the car are such as to require a permit, will require the Stewards to order either the permanent obliteration of the unauthorised displays or payment of a non-refundable fee which shall be not less than half the cost of the permit required for that event.

MINIMUM AGES

10.1. DRIVERS must be at least 17 years of age for all events using the public highway and all other events except:

Grass track, 2CV Cross and Mini Cross	16
Autotests, Production car or	
Sporting Trials	16
Karting (Short Circuit)	11

10.1.1. In the case of minors who cannot hold a licence to drive on the road, the MSA may require some evidence of an applicant's ability to drive.

10.2. NAVIGATOR (Non-driver)

Road rallies	14
Special stage rallies	16

10.3. All Competition Licence applications from minors must be supported by a parent or guardian as guarantor. Guarantors will be considered as the minor's entrant, and as such will be subject to the MSA Regulations.

10.4. A Kart driver who has not passed his or her 16th birthday is confined to races for drivers of a similar age group i.e. Juniors. The Date of Birth of such Junior must be entered on the Competition Licence.

10.5. A driver who is 17 years of age or over must have a valid driver's licence (not provisional) legally permitting him/her to drive a car on the public highway. Should this driver's licence be suspended or otherwise invalidated his/her Competition Licence must be returned to the MSA forthwith. The MSA may consider an application not to suspend the Competition Licence and to return it to its holder.

10.5.1. Drivers in those events which permit under 17 year-olds to compete, may continue to compete up to the age of 17 years and 6 months, whilst holding a Provisional Driving Licence.

10.5.2. Where a competitor is under the age of 17 the entry for an event must be supported by Parent or Guardian as Guarantor. Such Guarantor will be considered as being the 'Minors'

Entrant, and as such will be subject to these Regulations.

10.5.3. The Guarantor, or his representative must attend the event with the Minor, and sign on as his Entrant.

INDEMNITY AND UNDERTAKINGS

11.1. In consideration of The RAC Motor Sports Association Ltd granting a Competition Licence, the holder binds himself to the following requirements and undertakings:

(a) To abide by the MSA rules and any amendments or additions thereto which may be in force at any time that the licence is used for the purpose of taking part in a motor competition.

(b) To pay as liquidated damages for any breach of these Rules any sums awarded against him or the organisation which he represents within the maxima set out in the Rules.

(c) To save harmless and keep indemnified the MSA and such person, persons or body as may be authorised by the MSA to act on its behalf and/or to promote or organise the event in which he is participating and their respective officials, servants, representatives and agents from and against all actions, claims, costs, expenses and demands in respect of death or injury to himself howsoever caused arising out of or in connection with the entry or his taking part in this event and notwithstanding that the same may have been contributed to or occasioned by the negligence of the said bodies, their officials, servants, representatives or agents. Furthermore, in respect of any parts of an event on ground where third party insurance is not required by law this agreement shall in addition to the parties named above extend to all and any other competitor(s) and their servants and agents and to all actions, claims, costs, expenses and demands in respect of loss or damage to the person or property of himself, his driver(s), passenger(s) or mechanic(s).

(d) That to the best of the Licence holder's knowledge and belief the driver(s) possess(es) the standard of competence necessary for an event of the type to which an entry relates and that the vehicle entered is suitable and roadworthy for the event having regard to the course and the speeds which will be reached.

(e) That where appropriate, the use of the car entered shall be covered by insurance as required by the law, which is valid for such part of the event as shall take place on roads as defined by the law.

(f) That any driver, if so required by the MSA Regulations, undertakes to be in possession of a current certificate of Medical Fitness at the time of an event at which he is competing. Furthermore, should a driver at the time of any event be suffering from any disability whether permanent, or temporary which is likely to affect prejudicially his normal control of his automobile at the time of the event, he will not take part unless he has previously declared such disability to the MSA and has received permission to compete. A driver's medical attendant is automatically authorised to provide a medical practitioner acting for the MSA with such relevant information as he may require.

(g) That any application form for a licence which is signed by a person under the age of 18 years shall be countersigned by that person's parent or guardian, whose full name and address shall be given.

(h) The MSA recommends that Competitors should abstain from the consumption of alcohol or drugs before or during a competition.

FEES (VAT INCLUSIVE)

12.1. Licences – Car Driver/Entrant

	Rest	Nat	Int C	Int B	Int A
Race	£15.00	£23.00	£34.00	£45.00	£100.00
Speed	£8.00	£15.00	£24.00		
Rally	£8.00	£15.00	£28.00		
Historic Race			£34.00		

When two or more Driver/Entrant Licences for one person are applied for at the same time, the total fee will be that of the most expensive licence, plus half the cost of the other licence(s). This reduction will not apply to subsequent licences brought singly or to Clubman, Kart or Entrant Licences.

Clubman C	£4.00
Clubman RS	£11.00
Temporary	£6.50

12.2. Licences – Non/Driver

	Rest	Nat
Navigator	£8.00	£15.00

12.3. Licences – Trade Entrant

Kart	£16.00
Car	£35.00
Club	5 copies free of charge

(issued to Club Sec. or Comp. Sec. only).

12.4. Licences – Kart Driver/Entrant

	Novice	International
Kart (Short Circuit) (less than 1500m)	£4.00	£8.00
Kart (combined Long & Short Circuit) Licence	£6.00	£15.00

12.5. Upgrading Fee

The difference between the cost of the existing Licence and the new Licence plus £3.00

12.6. Advertising Permits

Restricted	£40.00
National	£80.00
International	£170.00

An Advertising Permit may be upgraded by returning the original adhesive disc, together with the difference in cost of the two permits.

Duplicates of Advertising Permits are not available.

12.7. Licence Copies or Duplicates

All copies or duplicates – £3.00 per copy.

12.8. Priority Issue

At all times 15 working days must be allowed for issue of a licence unless priority issue is specified. The charge for priority issue is £5.00. Use pre-addressed envelope and mark outside prominently with 'PRIORITY'.

12.9. Visa and Medical Expenses Insurance

Required before competing abroad and should be applied for before the Closing Date for the Event.
(£2,500 cover)

Entrant (no medical insurance)	£5.50
Entrant and Driver	£11.50
Entrant, Driver and Second Driver	£18.50
Visa Book	£57.50
Entrant and Driver (Karts)	£9.50
Surcharge if Visa is applied for after Closing Date	£20.00

13.1. An RAC Motor Sports Association Ltd Licence does not constitute Membership of the RAC Associates Section nor entitle Licence holders to the services provided by that section to their Members.

13.2. Licence holders are entitled by virtue of their licence fees to receive their licence certificate, the annual RAC British Motor Sports Yearbook and such other publications as the Association from time to time prepares for distribution.

APPLICATION FORMS

8301 All Licences and Advertising Permits.
CHEQUES AND OTHER FORMS OF MONEY ORDER MUST BE CROSSED AND MADE PAYABLE TO:
The RAC Motor Sports Association Ltd, 31 Belgrave Square, London SW1X 8QH.
(VAT No. 242 3048-95).

1983 RAC MOTOR SPORTS ASSOCIATION CHAMPIONSHIPS

Prospective contenders must register where appropriate a minimum of 7 days in advance of the first event in which a competitor wishes to claim points. Registration should be made on licence form 8301.

ACCEPTABLE LICENCES

	Closed (C)	Restricted (R)	National (N)	International (I)
Autocross		Speed R, N & I Rally R, N & I Clubman RS Temporary	Speed N & I Rally N & I	Speed I Rally I
Autotest	Club Card	Speed R, N & I Rally R, N & I Clubman C or RS Temporary	Speed N & I Rally N & I Clubman C or RS	Speed I Rally I
Circuit Race		Race R, N & I Kart I Historic Race	Race N & I	Race I
Drag Race		Speed R, N & I Race R, N & I Clubman RS Temporary	Speed N & I Race N & I Clubman RS	Speed I Race I
4 Wheel Drive	Club Card	Rally R, N & I Clubman C or RS Temporary	Rally N & I Clubman C or RS	Rally I
Grass Track Race		Speed R, N & I Race R, N & I Clubman RS Temporary	Speed N & I Race N & I	Speed I Race I
Hill Climb		Speed R, N & I Clubman RS Temporary	Speed N & I	Speed I
Historic Race		Historic Race Race R, N & I	Historic Race Race N & I	Historic Race Race I
Kart Race (Short Circuits)		Novice Kart Kart I Novice Kart SC Kart I SC	Kart I Kart I SC	Kart I Kart I SC
Kart Race (Long Circuits)		Novice Kart Kart I SC Kart I	Novice Kart Kart I SC Kart I	Kart I
Rally (driver)	Club Card	Rally R, N & I Clubman RS Temporary	Rally N & I	Rally I
Navigator (Non-driver)	Club Card	Navigator R & N Rally R, N & I Clubman RS Temporary	Navigator N Rally N & I	N/A
Rallycross		Speed R, N & I Rally R, N & I Clubman RS Temporary	Speed N & I Rally N & I	Speed I Rally I
Sand Race		Speed R, N & I Race R, N & I Clubman RS Temporary	Speed N & I Race N & I	Speed I Race I
Sprint		Speed R, N & I Clubman RS Temporary	Speed N & I	Speed I
Stock Car Racing		Speed R, N & I Race R, N & I Clubman RS Temporary	Speed N & I Race N & I	Speed I Race I
Trial, (Classic) (Production) (Sporting) (4W-D)	Club Card	Rally R, N & I Clubman C Clubman RS Temporary	Rally N & I Clubman C Clubman RS	Rally I

♛ MOTOR SPORTS RAC ASSOCIATION LIMITED

Application for 1983 Competition Licence

Surname *(see over)*

Forenames *(in full)*

Address *(to which licence should be sent)*

Postcode

Entrant's Address *(see over)*

Telephone number — Office

Home

Date of Birth

Passport Nationality

Town of Birth

Medical Declaration *(put X in box if required because of answers on reverse)* — YES

If you are over 17, do you hold a current licence to drive on the public highway (NOT Provisional)? — YES / NO

I enclose £5 extra for PRIORITY ISSUE — YES

I already hold 1983 Licence No.

I wish to apply for the following licences (please place X in appropriate box(es)). Please read Terms of Issue Form 8388 CAREFULLY before applying for any licence. ERRORS CANNOT BE RECTIFIED AFTER RECEIPT OF THIS FORM. Licences, other than temporary, are valid until 31st December 1983 only.

Car Licences

Race

International A	£100	RA
International B	£45	RB
International C	£34	RC
International Historic	£34	RH
National	£23	NR
Restricted	£15	RR

Speed

International	£24	IS
National	£15	NS
Restricted	£8	RS

Rally

International	£28	IY
National	£15	NY
Restricted	£8	RY

Navigator

National	£15	NN
Restricted	£8	RN

Clubmans

Clubmans RS	£11	CR
Clubmans C	£4	CC

Advertising Permit

International	£170	IP
National	£80	NP
Restricted	£40	RP

Entrants Licence

Valid for All Grades	£35	E

Kart Licences

International	£15	IK
International S/C	£8	SK
Novice	£6	NK
Novice S/C	£4	SN

Kart Entrants Licence

Valid for All Grades	£16	KE

Temporary Licence	£6.50	T

Valid from .... to ....

Note: Where one person applies for two or more licences on this form in the RACE/RALLY/SPEED categories the total fee will be the cost of the most expensive one plus half the cost of the other licence(s).
THIS DOES NOT APPLY TO ADVERTISING, KART, CLUBMANS OR ENTRANT LICENCES

Please register me for the Championship indicated (see over) — Championship _____

Fee _____ Make & Type of Car _____ Capacity _____

I have read and understood the terms of issue set out in Form 8388 and undertake to abide by them. I enclose cheque/postal orders crossed and made payable to The RAC Motor Sports Association Ltd for the sum of £ _____

If under 18 a Guarantor must also sign below stating relationship.

Applicants Signature _____

Guarantors Signature _____

Date _____

Relationship _____

THE MEDICAL DECLARATION ON THE BACK OF THIS FORM MUST BE COMPLETED

Notes

1. If this application is for an Entrants Licence in the name of a firm or organisation, enter that firms name on the line marked 'Surname'. The maximum number of words permitted in the title is six, continuing on the Forenames lines if necessary. The address should be that to which the licence, and all subsequent communications, should be sent. Insert the Entrants own address, if different, in the box marked 'Entrants Address'.

2. Please note that Licences can only be issued by post, and make allowance for delays of up to 15 working days. PRIORITY handling within three working days from time of receipt can be arranged for an extra fee of £5 provided the application is received by hand or Recorded Delivery. We regret that Licence queries cannot be dealt with by telephone but must be made in writing.

3. VAT at the standard rate is charged on a proportion of the licence fee only, and therefore this form should not be used as a VAT invoice.

Medical Declaration

The following must be completed by all applicants for a Drivers Licence (Car or Kart).

1. Name and address of your regular doctor

....

....

....

Answer Yes or No

2. Have you ever been rejected, or accepted at increased premium, for life insurance on medical grounds?

3. Have you ever been treated for, do you now have, or have you ever had, any of the following?

 (a) Nervous breakdown, mental disease, or disorder

 (b) Head injury with unconsciousness or concussion

 (c) Heart disease or disorder

 (d) High blood pressure

 (e) Diabetes

 (f) Dizziness, fainting spells, epilepsy, fits or blackouts

 (g) Have you ever had any disease, injury or operation to either eye?

 (h) Have you any abnormality of any part of the upper or lower limbs?

4. (a) Is your eyesight normal in both eyes?

 (b) If the answer to (4a) is NO — is your eyesight normal in both eyes with spectacles or other correction? If answer is still No, put X in Medical Declaration box overleaf.

5. (a) If immunised against tetanus, state date of immunisation

Date of Birth

Sex

 (i) I certify that the statements made to the MSA regarding my psychological and physical condition, and any previous illnesses, are true and accurate.

 (ii) I undertake that I will not use any drug considered to be illegal.

 (iii) I authorise any hospital or medical practitioner to furnish information relative to my medical condition to the Medical Committee.

If the answer to any of the above is YES please supply further details below and put X in Medical Declaration box overleaf.

Applicant's Signature _____

Date _____

RAC Championships

Indicate overleaf any championship you require to be registered for. The first column indicates the licence required.

RES	Autotest	£4
NAT	Leaders Hill Climb	£4
RES	Production Car Trial	£4
RES	Sporting Car Trial	£4
RES	Drag Racing	£4
NAT	Sprint	£4
NAT	Leaders Sprint	£4
NAT	Rallycross	£4

NAT	Hill Climb	£5
INT	British Saloon Car – Drivers	£6
INT	British Saloon Car – Manufacturers	£6

NB. It is not possible to register in both the Hill Climb and Leaders Hill Climb or the Sprint and Leaders Sprint Championship at the same time. Manufacturers wishing to claim points in the Manufacturers British Saloon Car Championship will be required to register each type of car.

Return this form, with appropriate remittance to The RAC Motor Sports Association Ltd, 31 Belgrave Square, London SW1X 8QH. For further information consult Licence Information Form 8388, copies on request.

Form 8301

APPENDIX 3
Specimen rally paperwork

Presents the

di Plenti Rally

B.T.R.D.A. SILVER STAR
A.N.C.C.

Road Rally Championships

TRACKROD MOTOR CLUB LIMITED

SHELLSPORT COSTA DI PLENTI RALLY

28th/29th MARCH, 1981

ADDITIONAL SUPPLEMENTARY REGULATIONS

1 TRACKROD MOTOR CLUB LTD. will promote a restricted permit rally on 28th/29th March, 1981. The event will be governed by the General Competition Rules, Standing Supplementary Regulations of the R.A.C. incorporating the provisions of the International Sporting Code of the F.I.A. These A.S.R.'s and any written instructions the promoters may issue for the event. The event will be sponsored by SHELL OIL U.K. and will be a qualifying event for the Motoring News/B.T.R.D.A. Silver Star and A.N.C.C. Road Rally Championships.

2 PERMITS

R.A.C. permit No. .... has been issued.
D.O.E. authorisation No. .... has been issued.
Club Registration No. 1230

3 ELIGIBILITY

The event is open to:-
a) All fully elected members of the promoting club.
b) Members of the Association of Northern Car Clubs, and the B.T.R.D.A. who hold a competition licence valid for the event. Club Membership Cards and Competition Licences will be inspected at signing on. Where applicable, Advertising Permits and Entrants Licences will also be inspected.

4 START and FINISH

The event will start at Croft and Blackburn Limited, MR 104/310516 and finish at The Post House, Bramhope, MR 104/249435½. The first car will start at 23.31 Hrs. Any competitor not signed on 2 hrs before their due start time will be excluded and the place offered to the highest placed reserve present. Individual times of starting will be notified in the final instructions.

5 ROUTE and FUEL

The Route will be of approximately 180 miles on all types of road. Petrol will be available at the start and after approx. 90 miles. FIVE STAR will NOT be available.

6 MAPS

The route will be contained on Map Nos. 98, 99 and 104, 1:50,000 latest editions.

FOREWORD

On behalf of Trackrod Motor Club Limited, We invite you to compete in this, the seventh Shellsport Costa Di Plenti Rally. The Rally will keep to the successful format of previous years, a mixture of Selectives and Time Control sections

Thanks to the increased generosity of Shell U.K. Oil and our advertisers we are able to maintain our wide spread of prize money and awards.

We are pleased to announce that we are once again in the Motoring News/ B.T.R.D.A. Silver Star and A.N.C.C. Championships.

We wish you all an enjoyable and successful rally.

Competition for entries is expected to be fierce, need we say more !!!

The Organisers

10 AWARDS

The following awards will be presented:

1st Overall	The Square & Compass Rosebowl to Driver
	The Trackrod Trophy to Navigator and replicas plus £50 cash
2nd Overall	The Chubb Trophy to Driver, The Tetley Bittermen Trophy to Navigator and replicas plus £40 cash
1st Expert	The Nationwide Award and replicas to Driver and Navigator, plus £25 cash
2nd Expert	An award to Driver and Navigator plus £20 cash
3rd Expert	An award to Driver and Navigator plus £15 cash
4th Expert	An award to Driver and Navigator
1st Semi Expert	The Costa Trophy and replicas to Driver and Navigator plus £25 cash
2nd Semi Expert	An award to Driver and Navigator plus £20 cash
3rd Semi Expert	An award to Driver and Navigator plus £15 cash
4th Semi Expert	An award to Driver and Navigator
1st Novice	The Nil Desperandum Trophy and replicas to Driver and Navigator plus £25 cash
2nd Novice	An award to Driver and Navigator plus £20 cash
3rd Novice	An award to Driver and Navigator plus £15 cash
4th Novice	An award to Driver and Navigator
Best Performance by a Non-sponsored Crew	The Hepolite Glacier Trophy presented by A.E. Autoparts Limited and Replicas
Best Ford (Non-sponsored)	The Tate Trophy and replicas
Best British Leyland	The Coopers of Oulton Trophy and replicas
Best Chrysler	The Slaid Hill Motors Trophy and replicas
Best Vauxhall	The Glanfield Lawrence Trophy and replicas
Best under 1300 c.c.	The Vehicles For Fun (VFF) and replicas
Best Mixed Crew or All Ladies	An award to each crew member
Best Non-Finisher to Halfway	Expert - a unique award
	Semi-Expert - a unique award
	Novice - a unique award
Best Trackrod Member not winning another award	The Mr. & Mrs. D. Parsons Trophy and replicas
Team Award	An award to each member of the best team

No crew may win more than one award except team awards.
Additional awards will be notified in the final instructions.
All major trophies are the property of Trackrod Motor Club Limited, and must be returned after 11 months or before the next Costa di Plenty Rally, whichever is the sooner.

7 IDENTIFICATION

The organisers will supply the rally plates. Competition numbers will be on sale at the start. The rally plates will be displayed at the front and rear of the vehicle. The black competition numbers will be affixed on a white background on either side of the car. (SSR BB/(t) applies). All such identification must be carried throughout the event and immediately removed or covered on finishing or retiring from the event.

8 SCRUTINEERING

Scrutineering will commence at 20.00 hrs. Your individual times of scrutineering will be advised in the final instructions.

Cars must be presented for scrutineering as near as possible to the time stated in the final instructions. Cars will be examined for their general roadworthiness and will be required to comply with R.A.C. SSR's and Vehicle Regulations. These Regulations will be strictly adhered to.

Vehicles registered for the B.T.R.D.A. 1300 class will also be checked for eligibility.

Competitors are also reminded of the recommendations of Vehicle Regulations HH.

Vehicles will be inspected for damage at the start, half-way and finish of the event.

Competitors will be required to complete a damage declaration form at the end of the event. Failure to complete this form or failure to report any damage he or she may have caused will result in exclusion from the results and the incident will be reported to the R.A.C., A.N.C.C. and other organisers.

Competitors who retire during the event must complete and return this form to the organisers i.e. The Secretary of the Meeting, within three days of the event. Failure to do so will result in the actions listed above. A noise check will take place at the start and en route. Cars exceeding 75 dB at 5,000 r.p.m. when stationary, 7 metres from the mid point of the car will not be allowed to start, or continue.

9 CLASSES

The event will consist of the following classes:-

1) Expert: A crew in which either member has finished in the top 10 of a restricted rally or the top three of a closed joint rally (excluding novice rallies).

2) Semi-Expert: A crew in which either member has finished in the top 15 of a restricted rally or the top 10 of a closed joint, and does not qualify for expert Excluding novice rallies.

3) Novice: Any crew who do not qualify for expert or semi-expert classes as defined above. But have finished at least 2 restricted rallies, excluding novice rallies.

Team entries comprising of three cars will be accepted up to the start of the event. The organisers reserve the right to re-classify any crew and no protest will be allowed on this point.

11 ENTRIES

a) The maximum entry for the event is 90, the minimum is 70. Should this figure not be reached the organisers reserve the right to cancel the event. If the entry limit is reached before closing date, 10 reserve entries for each class will be accepted. Any reserve entry who signs the starters sheet by 21.30 hrs. and is not offered a starting number by the promoters will be entitled to a refund of their entry fee.

b) Allocation of Entries: All entries must be made on an Official Entry Form and accompanied by the appropriate fees. Telephoned entries will NOT be accepted. All entries will be allocated on a class basis, strictly on date of receipt of entry. Except for 10 entries which may be allocated at the organisers discretion.

c) In order to qualify for a refund of entry fee, entrants must notify in writing their intentions of withdrawal of entry on or before Friday, 20th March, 1981. Refund of entry fees in whole or part after this date will be at the discretion of the organisers.

d) The entry list opens on publication of these regulations and closes finally on Monday, 23rd March, 1981. The entry fee is £20.00. Team entries will be £3.00 per three car team.

12 OFFICIALS

The Entries Secretary to whom all entries must be sent is:-
Mrs. Rebecca Kemp, 67 Allerton Grange Way, Leeds, LS17 6LR.
Telephone Leeds (0532) 683156

Other senior Officials are:
Secretary of the Meeting: T.B.A.
Clerks of the Course:
Martin S. Kemp, 67 Allerton Grange Way, Leeds, LS17 6LR
Steven Mills

Chief Marshals:
Gez Waters, 4 Thorn Grove, Leeds, LS8 3LY. Tel. Leeds 651436 (H)
John Westmorland, 46 Hillcrest, Tadcaster, N. Yorks. Tel. Tad. 833064 (H)
Chief Timekeeper: Steven Mills
Event Stewards: T.B.A.
Chief Scrutineers: Barry Dove and Team
Public Relations: Mike Robson, John Burdon and Team
Results Controllers: C.S.M.A. Nottingham Group
A.N.C.C. Observer: T.B.A:

13 ORDER OF STARTING

This will be at the organisers discretion, based on previous rally results as stated on the entry form.

14 ROAD BOOK

Entrants will be supplied with a Road Book 1 hour before their due start time. This document will provide all the information necessary to enable competitors to comply with SSR. S38 , Blackspots, Q.Z.'s etc will be available with the road book.

15 MODIFICATIONS TO SSR's

All SSR's of the R.A.C. apply as written except for the following, which are modified:

P40 Teams
Competitors may belong to more than one team.

S18 & S22 Signs
All official signs will have mandatory authority.
Examples of such signs will be displayed at the start.

S36 Checks.
The organisers may establish a check at any point for the purpose of observing maintenance of a set speed and/or time schedule and/or route.

S40 Three Quarter Time
S40 will not apply at the petrol halt.

S47 Timing
Certain sections of the route will be timed to the previous complete second. These will be indicated in the Road Book.

S50 & S51 Not applicable

S60 Lateness
Competitors will reduce all lateness at the petrol halt

S68 Performance
The fails system will apply

a)	as defined		1 Fail
b)	as defined		1 Fail
c)	as defined		1 Fail
d)	as defined		1 Fail
e) to k)	Not applicable		
l)	as defined		2 Marks
m)	as defined /minute		1 Mark
	/sec.		1/60th Mark
			1 Fail/minute
n)	as defined		
o)	as defined)		
p)	as defined)	1st offence	1 Fail
q)	as defined)	2nd offence	Exclusion
r)	As defined + "or the use of lights in a non-competitive section"		
		1st offence	1 Fail
		2nd offence	Exclusion
s)	as defined	1st offence	1 Fail
		2nd offence	Exclusion
t)	Not applicable		
u)	as defined	1st offence	Exclusion
v)	as defined		
w)	Observed in an O. O. Bounds area specified O.O. Bounds - Exclusion		

S23 Standing Give Ways
as defined   1st offence   Exclusion

16 NAVIGATION

The correct route will be the shortest route by any road marked on the map, between controls avoiding non-goers and out of bounds areas, complying with the road book. If any road marked on the map as a footpath, or not at all, is to be used, details will be given in the Road Book.

24 PREVIOUS WINNERS

1973	The Arab Oil Sheiks	Escort Mexico
1974	Ken Goodall/Mike Tempest	Firenza
1975	Ron Ship/Don Davidson	Opel Ascona
1976	Vincent Girardier/Bill Kilpatrick	Very Quick Escort !
1977	Bob Bean/Nigel Raeburn	RS2000
1978	Tony Revell/Dave Taylor	
1979	10' Snow Banks	
1980	Ron Beecroft/John Millington	Talbot Sunbeam 2 litre

25 INSURANCE

Members will be aware that most policies no longer cover competitive events, but arrangements have been offered by the R.A.C.'s brokers, Messrs. C. T. Bowring (London) Limited, to give, subject to an acceptable proposal, Third Party Cover for £9.00. AS PASSENGER LIABILITY COVER IS MANDATORY ON OR AFTER 1st DECEMBER, 1972. LETTERS OF ACCEPTANCE BEARING THE PREFIX "ANC" WILL BE INVALID. DRIVERS MUST THEREFORE OBTAIN A NEW LETTER OF ACCEPTANCE BEARING PREFIX "RDS" BY SUBMITTING A NEW PROPOSAL THROUGH THE ORGANISING CLUB IN THE USUAL WAY.

Entrants wishing to avail themselves of this offer must apply with their entry form for a proposal form and should note that this must be returned *fully completed* to the Secretary of the Meeting not less than eighteen days before the event.

All correspondence must be undertaken by the club, The Brokers cannot treat direct with individual drivers either by correspondence or telephone.

Drivers who have already completed a Proposal Form for events since 1st December, 1972, Should quote the reference number shown on their Letter of Acceptance, *Which must be produced to a club official* when paying the premium, before the event takes place.

Confirmation of cover - subject to the payment of premium, which must be paid before the start - will be indicated with Final Instructions to individual competitors. In the (we hope) unlikely event of any proposal not being acceptable, the competitor should immediately contact his own Insurers, as the promoter cannot undertake to accept this as a reason for return of entry fee.

IT IS VITAL THAT ENTRANTS WISHING TO EFFECT THIS FORM OF INSURANCE COMPLY STRICTLY WITH THE TIMETABLE INDICATED.

17 TIMING

Timing will be by marshals watches on the TARGA system. Timing will be to the previous whole minute except on certain sections where timing will be to the previous whole second.

18 CONTROLS

a) All time controls will be manned.
b) Passage checks may be manned. In the event of a check being unmanned, a code board will be substituted and the code should be recorded on the time card. In both cases a signature will be required at the next time control as proof of passage.
c) Competitors will be required to sign in receipt of times given at selective starts and finishes.
d) Non-competitive Sections, May be defined as a link section between two competitive sections. In these sections noise must be kept to a minimum and auxiliary lights extinguished. These sections will be defined in the Road Book. Competitors are reminded that time must NOT be made up in these sections. The average speed for such a section will not exceed 20 m.p.h.

19 TIMES and MILEAGES

All official times and mileages will be deemed correct.

20 LATENESS

Any competitor visiting a control 31 or more minutes after his due time will be deemed not to have visited that control.

21 NOISE

Marshals will be stationed in Non Competitive Sections and penalties under A.S.R. 15 will be rigidly enforced.
All will be strictly marshalled by Judges of Fact, qualified to carry out their duties, either by experience or noise meters. Should a competitor's exhaust system become damaged en route any marshal in charge of a control or check is empowered to withhold the competitor's time card until the damage is rectified to his satisfaction. No time will be allowed for any delay resulting from such repair.

22 RESULTS and PRIZEGIVING

Provisional Results will be published as soon as possible after the event. Protests must be made in accordance with SSR P47(a).
No telephone enquiries as to results will be entertained.
Prizegiving will take place as soon as possible after the results have been declared final.

23 BREAKFAST

Breakfast is available at the finish and need not be ordered.

TRACKROD MOTOR CLUB LTD.

Shell SPORT

COSTA DI PLENTI '81

28th/29th March 1981

Entry Form

Entries Secretary:-

---

* Delete as applicable

ENTRANT

Full Name ....

Address .... Tel. No. ....

Comp. Licence No. ....

DRIVER

Full Name ....

Address ....

Tel. No. .... Comp. Licence No. ....

Club ....

NAVIGATOR

Full Name ....

Address ....

Tel. No. .... Comp. Licence No. ....

Club ....

CAR

Make.. Model...............

Engine Capacity............................ Registration No...........

INSURANCE

* RDS No. .... / I require a proposal form / I have a private

insurance with ....
(Name and Address of Company)

....

On Policy No. ....

CHAMPIONSHIP CONTENDERS

	Driver		Nav.	
		Reg. No.		Reg. No.
B.T.R.D.A.				
A.N.C.C.				
H.M.S.G.				
B.T.R.D.A. 1300				

INDEMNIFICATION

I have read the supplementary regulations issued for this event and agree to be bound by them and by the General Competition Rules of the Royal Automobile Club. In consideration of the acceptance of this entry or of my being permitted to take part in this event. I agree to save harmless and keep indemnified the Royal Automobile Club, such person, persons or body as may be authorised by the Royal Automobile Club to promote or organise this event and their respective officials, servants, representatives and agents from and against all actions, claims, costs, expenses and demands in respect of death or injury to myself, howsoever caused arising out of or in connection with this entry or my taking part in this event, and notwithstanding that the same may have been contributed to or occasioned by the negligence of the said bodies, their officials, servants, representatives or agents other than the negligence of servants of the Royal Automobile Club on duties not connected with the said event.

Furthermore, in respect of any parts of this event on ground where third party insurance is not required by law this agreement shall in addition to the parties named above extend to all and any other competitor/s and their servants and agents to all actions, claims, costs, expenses and demands in respect of loss or damage to the person or property of myself, my driver(s), passenger(s) or mechanic(s) but shall not extend to a competitor adjudged guilty of reckless driving under the said General Competition Rules.

Driver's Signature ....

My age is .... (if applicable state 'over 17 years')

Navigator's Signature ....

My age is .... (if applicable state 'over 17 years')

I declare that the use of the car hereby entered is covered by insurance as required by the law, which is valid for such part of this event as shall take part on roads as defined in that Act.

Entrant's Signature ....

My age is .... (if applicable state 'over 17 years')

If the Entrant is under 18 years of age, this form must be countersigned by a Parent or Guardian.

Signed .... Parent/Guardian

Name (in full) of Parent/Guardian ....

Address ....

PAST BEST PERFORMANCE ON RALLIES

Class Entered [ ] (Insert 1, 2, 3)

Event	Year	Status	Result O/A & Class

FEES - Make cheques payable to:- Trackrod Motor Club Rally Account
✦ Team Entries - Please enclose details if known - or enter on day

Entry Fee at £20.00 ....

✦ Team Entries at £3.00 ....

Trackrod Membership £4.00 per person ....

RDS Insurance at £9.00 ....

TOTAL

PLEASE ADDRESS ALL THE LABELS AND ENCLOSE

For official use only

R.E.C.	Sig.	Det.	Ins.	Cash	File No.	Seed

FURNESS DISTRICT MOTOR CLUB LTD
1981 MOTORING NEWS CHAMPIONSHIP ROUND 9

THE
R.L.BROWN
TROPHY RALLY
19th/20th SEPTEMBER 1981

G & E BENSON LTD Vauxhall/Opel Dealer
GRIZEBECK SERVICE STATION   CUMBRIA

1980 Winners Terry Benson Chris Pudsey

Best MN/BTRDA Event of 1980 awarded the Tyler Morris Trophy

Right panel (Final Instructions — Continued)

[Final Instructions - Continued]

[7] [ROUTE CUTTING]

On this event Competitors who (for whatever reasons) are forced to cut part of the route to remain within maximum permitted lateness will be penalised in accordance with the penalties in Section 19 of the Supplementary Regulations, except for S.R. 1.4.13.5(n) which will not apply in the above circumstances.

[8] [AMENDMENTS TO S.Rs]

    Penalties   S.R. 19(m) - Arriving at a Main Time Control over 45 mins 59 secs
                            after due time = EXCLUSION.

    Insurance   S.R. 31 - After consultation with
                            C.T. Bowring we have been advised NOT to visually
                            check insurance policies for Road Traffic Act
                            requirements - this is the Competitor's responsibility.
    We do insist, however, that all Competitors sign the indemnification on the Entry
    Form relating to insurance. Those using the R.D.S. Scheme must produce their
    Letters of Acceptance and those using private insurance must give the name
    and address of their insurers and their policy number, and must also produce
    proof of rally cover.

    *   *   *   *   *   *   *   *   *

* MAY WE ON BEHALF OF FURNESS DISTRICT MOTOR CLUB LTD WISH YOU ALL AN ENJOYABLE
              AND SUCCESSFUL "R.L. BROWN '81".   [THE ORGANISERS]

DVB ....   [FOR YOUR USE] ....

[N O T E S]   .... (Route amendments, additional regulations, etc, etc) =

Left panel (Final Instructions)

[F I N A L   I N S T R U C T I O N S]

R.A.C. Permit Number   [RAL 19698]   D.o.E. Number [   ]

* YOUR
  RALLY =   [2 7 .]   [Seeding is a difficult task - we are satisfied
  NUMBER   that we have done our best with the information
                             both given and known.]

Your
Start Time   [2 3 . 2 3 .]   Report to the   [1 9 . 2 7 .]
is =   Noise Check   [DO NOT REPORT BEFORE THIS
                                     at =   TIME - YOU WILL BE TURNED
                                                            AWAY IF YOU DO !]

[1] [NOISE CHECK]

    Report to the Marshal at mapref 96|25738494.
    (Kirkby Quarry Road End) who will direct you to the Noise Check.
    Give the Noise Marshal your Scrutineering Check Card - he will then mark your
    decibel reading on it. (Maximum permitted level = 78 dB @ 5000 rpm).

[2] [SCRUTINEERING]

    From the Noise Check proceed to Benson's Garage, Grizebeck, at mapref 96|23885.
    Fill up with petrol, oil, etc, before Scrutineering. Follow Marshals' instructions
    to the Scrutineering Area.

[3] [SIGNING & DOCUMENTATION]

    After successfully completing Scrutineering proceed to the Start at the Ecole
    Riggs Hotel, nr Broughton-in-Furness, at mapref 96|211865.
    Drive with CARE when approaching the Hotel. Report to the Marshal who will give
    you directions for parking.
    Signing-on and Documentation will take place inside the Hotel. You will be
    required to produce =

    [i]   Club Membership Cards.   [iii] Insurance Certificates.
    [ii] Competition Licences.   [iv] Entrant's Licence/Advertising Permit
                                             [where applicable]

    If you fail to produce your documents YOU WILL NOT BE ALLOWED TO START.

    Competition Numbers, Maps, Romers and all Rally Aids will be on sale at the Start
    from Roger Gosh's "Rally Aids".

[4] [PETROL]

    Petrol will be available as follows =
      (a) At Scrutineering.
      (b) After approximately 55 miles.
      (c) After approximately 60 miles.
      (d) At Benson's Garage, Grizebeck, after the Rally - from 09-00 hours.
    A night service is available at the Shell Garage, Greenodd, at mapref 96|310264.

[5] [TRAILER PARKING]

    Trailers may be parked at the Ecole Riggs Hotel at the owner's responsibility.
    An area has been allocated for this purpose - DO NOT PARK without first consulting the
    Marshal on duty at the Start.

[6] [MEDICAL ASSISTANCE]

    If, after an accident, URGENT medical aid is required, a Red Cross Card (supplied
    by the Organisers) should be displayed (i.e. waved about). Competitors seeing one of
    these cards being displayed should stop at the scene of the accident, ascertain what
    assistance is required, render any help possible, and then report the facts to the
    Marshal at the next Control.
    Any Competitor who, through assisting in this way, is delayed, should report the
    facts to the Organisers. The Organisers may grant a time allowance at their discretion,
    if they are satisfied that the claim is genuine.
    The penalty for displaying the Red Cross Card when URGENT medical assistance is
    NOT required is = EXCLUSION.   [CONTINUED ....]

BRECON OLD FORGE GARAGE MOTOR CLUB 'GREMLIN' Rally

Car No.	Driver/Navigator	Position Class	Overall
2	B Gwynne/P Watkins	3rd	4th
4	R Beecroft/J Millington	1st	1st
6	R Morus/B Foster	5th	2nd
8	M Hutchinson/M Harris	2nd	6th
14	D Carlsen/P Forrester		3rd
15	R Platt/P Gray	6th	7th
16	R Price/R Leakey	4th	5th
18	J Edwards-Parton/D Davidson	7th	8th
23	E Evans/E Evans		18th
24	T Hill/A Tomkinson		11th
25	M Watkins/M Lenchars	10th	10th
27	J Hodge/M Howard	9th	16th
28	J Cakebread/J Savage	8th	9th
37	J Butson/T Turner		20th

CLASS 2

Car No.	Driver/Navigator	Position Class	Overall
43	M Wakefield/R Allam	3rd	14th
51	E Park/G Morgan		17th
54	R Kelsall/T Johnson		25th
58	D Wooton/D Finnegan		15th
99	M Vaughan/M Greenland		19th
101	H Thomas/M Jaffa		13th
104	B Earland/D Meadows	2nd	13th
105	B France/G Reuter	1st	12th
107	R Read/D Hopkins		26th
109	T Turner/T Wray		23rd
112	R Sharpley/D Bennett		24th
114	B Beeden/B Hazelhurst		30th
116	M Lawrence/M A W Brown		27th
118	D Simmonds/M Andrews		31st
120	D Astrobus/A Bowden		21st
124	D Hancock/B Hancock		29th
126	D Pollia/G Kamonda		28th

CLASS 3

Car No.	Driver/Navigator	Position Class	Overall
134	R Johnson/B Bower	3rd	
141	P Jukes/B Proctor	2nd	
142	G Griffith/P Jones	1st	

APPENDIX 4
Route cards

To be issued at start

SCORPION RALLY 1973

START		484674		
		467½678		
		480½749	WNW	
TC.1	E	465765		Car 0 due 22.47
TC.8	N	492805		Car 0 due 23.31
TC.14	ENE	370½872½		Car 0 due 01.16
TC.19	SE	273½843	NW	Car 0 due 01.52

First half road-books should be handed in here. For the purposes of qualifying as a finisher, crews must hand in there road book and visit the control within 30 minutes of their due time. From TC.19 travel quietly to take in petrol at 235886½. Please be especially quiet in Shrivenham and at the garage. Then return along the B.4000 to TC.20 — great care, 2 way rally traffic. At TC.20 please pull on to the grass verge and park as directed by the marshal. All lateness should be absorbed at TC.20.

TC.20	NNW	236½840		Car 0 due 02.45
TC.24	NE	321779		Car 0 due 03.06
TC.28	SE	292683		Car 0 due 03.40
TC.33	NW	290635		Car 0 due 04.13
TC.44	NW	414586	SE	Car 0 due 05.29

To qualify as a finisher, crews should visit TC.44 within 30 minutes of their due time.

From TC.44 crews should travel quietly to the finish at 484674 and hand in their second half time card to the Marshal.

From TC.13 travel very quietly through Upper Basildon, then via W616781 NW, and quietly through Streatley to the start of the first selective.

SELECTIVE 1	START		572837	SW	Car 0 due 00.24
	via		544826	SSW	
	PC.7	NNE	540815	SSW	Care – this junction is not as map and will be arrowed.
	via		534805½	N	
	PC.8	SSW	535820	SW	
	FINISH	ESE	527823½	W	Time allowed 10 minutes

It is very rough to the start of Selective 2.

SELECTIVE 2	START	E	520823	NW	Car 0 due 00.43
	via		506823	NW	Bump as you leave the tarmac.
	PC.9	SE	500829	N	Yes – its an unmarked track. Don't worry its simple when you get there.
	via	NNE	492¾833¾	NW	
	FINISH	NE	491834¼		Time allowed – 5 minutes

Care turning right onto A34, then via 478½892 to TC.13A at ENE 416½884. From TC.13A, via 403½879½ SSW, to TC.14 you must travel very quietly through Wantage. You have plenty of time and are not allowed to make up any time.

SELECTIVE 3	START	SW	372586	NE	Car 0 due 05.17
	via		379592½	NE	Care of the ruts
	via	W	398620	SE	
	FINISH	NW	414586	SE	Time allowed – 12 minutes

"THE R.L. BROWN TROPHY RALLY '81"

Route Card

1

CONTROL	MAP REFERENCE	APPROACH	DEPART	TIME	COMMENTS
M.T.C.1	96|210½865½	–	SW	–	Standard Time 22.56 hrs

* Non-Competitive Section M.T.C. 1 to C.S. 1 – STOP at junction with main road when leaving Hotel grounds – Quiet FOXFIELD – Level Crossing 210½851¾

CONTROL	MAP REFERENCE	APPROACH	DEPART	TIME	COMMENTS
C.S. 1	211½850	NW	SE	4	Level Crossing 214 847¼
C.F. 1	232¼838¼	W	SE	4	

* Non-Competitive Section C.F. 1 to C.S. 2 – STOP and Quiet at junction with A595 – STOP at junction with A5092

CONTROL	MAP REFERENCE	APPROACH	DEPART	TIME	COMMENTS
C.S. 2	256 848½	NE	SW	4	Drive with care – VERY DEEP DROPS adjacent to road through quarry – refer to Tulip Diagram
C.F. 2	239½827	NNE	SSW	4	

* Non-Competitive Section C.F. 2 to C.S. 3 – Strict Quiet BECKSIDE

CONTROL	MAP REFERENCE	APPROACH	DEPART	TIME	COMMENTS
C.S. 3	238 819	N	SSE	4	Beware of sheep on road !
C.F. 3	274½833	SW	NW	8	

* Non-Competitive Section C.F. 3 to C.S. 4 – STOP at junction with A5092

CONTROL	MAP REFERENCE	APPROACH	DEPART	TIME	COMMENTS
C.S. 4	260 851	SE	NW	4	Beware of sheep on road !
C.F. 4	275½863	WNW	ESE	5	

* Non-Competitive Section C.F. 4 to C.S. 5 – Strict Quiet KENDALL GROUND FARM – Out-of-Bounds 50m, radius of 287 855¼ – STOP at junction with A5092

CONTROL	MAP REFERENCE	APPROACH	DEPART	TIME	COMMENTS
C.S. 5	295 850	NE	SW	5	
C.F. 5	307 817	N	S	7	

* Non-Competitive Section C.F. 5 to C.S. 6 – STOP at junction with A590 – STOP at junction with ARRAD FOOT by-pass [not shown on map] 310 811 – New road to GREENODD very similar to A590 as shown on map

CONTROL	MAP REFERENCE	APPROACH	DEPART	TIME	COMMENTS
C.S. 6	343½828	N	S	9	
P.C. 'A'	386½810¼	SW	E		
P.C. 'B'	395 815½	S	NE		Out-of-Bounds 200 m, radius of
P.C. 'C'	389½826½	S	W		390½816
C.F. 6	383 843½	S	N	15	

* Non-Competitive Section C.F. 6 to C.S. 7 – STOP at junction with A590 – Out-of-Bounds 50m, radius of 397 836

CONTROL	MAP REFERENCE	APPROACH	DEPART	TIME	COMMENTS
C.S. 7	399 837½	SW	NE	4	
P.C. 'D'	406 832½	SW	NE		Severe downhill hairpins 410½635 to 'X'-rds
P.C. 'E'	415 870	SE	WNW		
C.F. 7	417¾878¾	W	NE	11	

CONTINUED PAGE 2

[1]

"THE R.L. BROWN TROPHY RALLY '81"
Route Card

CONTROL	MAP REFERENCE	APPROACH	DEPART	TIME	COMMENTS
* Non-Competitive Section C.F. 7 to C.S. 14 to C.G. 14 - STOP at junction with A593 - Strict Quiet LITTLE LANGDALE - please drive on DIPPED lights through village					
C.S. 14	298 032	ENE	SSW	7	
C.F. 14	296 018	NE	SW	6	Beware of sheep on road :
* Non-Competitive Section C.F. 14 to C.S. 15					
C.S. 15	245 013½	SW	SW	4	Beware of sheep on road :
C.F. 15	96 231 943	NNE	SSW	8	
* Non-Competitive Section C.F. 15 to C.S. 16 - Quiet SEATHWAITE - Quiet HALL DUNNERDALE					
C.S. 16	211 050½	NE	SSW	4	Beware of sheep on road :
P.C. 'K'	239 919½	NW	SW		
C.F. 16	269 933½	WNW	ESE	15	
* Non-Competitive Section C.F. 16 to C.S. 17					
C.S. 17	248 003	NW	SE	6	Beware of sheep on road :
C.F. 17	239 852	NNE	SSE	7	
* Non-Competitive Section C.F. 17 to M.T.C. 3 (IN) - STOP at junction with A5092					
M.T.C.3 (IN)	238 850½	NNE	-	4	HAND IN TIME CARD 2
* This Section M.T.C. 3 (IN) to M.T.C. 3 (OUT) is a Rest Halt and lateness can be reduced					
M.T.C.3 (OUT)	237 851½	-	NNW	9	Standard Time 03.30 hrs
* Non-Competitive Section M.T.C. 3 (OUT) to C.S. 18					
C.S. 18	233 866½	SW	NE	4	White no-go 234 895 :
P.C. 'L'	231 897	NE	SW		
P.C. 'M'	228 897	S	N		
C.F. 18	231 894	NW	SSE	8	
* Non-Competitive Section C.F. 18 to C.S. 19 - STOP at junction with A593 - STOP at junction with A595 - Junction with A595 not as map - STOP signs precede Give Way by 40 metres - STOP AT BOTH JUNCTIONS					
C.S. 19	197 881½	SE	NW	5	Beware of sheep on road :
C.F. 19	187 242½	W	NE	7	
* Non-Competitive Section C.F. 19 to C.S. 20 - STOP at junction 196 930½ - Strict Quiet ULPHA					

CONTINUED PAGE 4

[2]

"THE R.L. BROWN TROPHY RALLY '81"
Route Card

CONTROL	MAP REFERENCE	APPROACH	DEPART	TIME	COMMENTS
* Non-Competitive Section C.F. 7 to C.S. 8 - Strict Quiet WOODSIDE COTTAGE 426 895					
C.S. 8	425 897	S	SW	4	Out-of-Bounds G.S. 4291 FORD at 413 918½
C.F. 8	409 916½	NE	SW	9	
* Non-Competitive Section C.F. 8 to M.T.C. 2 (IN) - STOP at junction with A592 - Stop at junction with A590					
M.T.C.2 (IN)	375 856	NW	-	8	HAND IN TIME CARD 1
* This Section M.T.C. 2 (IN) to M.T.C. 2 (OUT) is a Rest Halt and lateness can be reduced					
M.T.C.2 (OUT)	375 856	-	NW	15	Standard Time 01.00 hrs
* Non-Competitive Section M.T.C. 2 (OUT) to C.S. 9					
C.S. 9	366 863½	NE	SW	4	
P.C. 'G'	358 863½	ESE	SSW		
P.C. 'H'	353 859	ESE	WNW		
C.F. 9	342 886½	S	NW	6	
* Non-Competitive Section C.F. 9 to C.S. 10 - Strict Quiet HUSLAND - Quiet CROSSLANDS					
C.S. 10	345 894½	W	NE	4	
C.F. 10	369 937	S	N	7	
* Non-Competitive Section C.F. 10 to C.S. 11 - Strict Quiet EEL HOUSE					
C.S. 11	367 942	SE	NW	4	
P.C. 'I'	339 897½	N	WSW		
P.C. 'J'	332 893½	ENE	NNE		
C.F. 11	331 892½	W	SW	16	
* Non-Competitive Section C.F. 11 to C.S. 12 - Quiet WHITESTOCK HALL - Quiet OXEN PARK					
C.S. 12	317 810	NE	SW	4	Out-of-Bounds G.S. 3088
C.F. 12	310 904	NE	SW	25	
* Non-Competitive Section C.F. 12 to C.S. 13 - Out-of-Bounds 200 m. radius of 304 980 - White road through HIGH WATERHEAD rough in places - timing relaxed - White no-go at 314 994 - STOP at junction with A593					
C.S. 13	314 998	S	NNE	4	Out-of-Bounds 200 m. radius of 901 316 028
C.F. 13	901 308 021½	NW	NE	6	

CONTINUED PAGE 3

"THE R.L. BROWN TROPHY RALLY '81"

Route Card

CONTROL	MAP REFERENCE	APPROACH	DEPART	TIME	COMMENTS
C.S. 30	195 940	SE	N.	4	Beware of sheep on road !
C.F. 30	114 944	N	S	12	
* Non-Competitive Section C.F. 30 to C.S. 31 – STOP at junction with A595
C.S. 31	116 940	N.	SE	4	Beware of sheep on road !
C.F. 31	184 977	NW	SE	13	
* Non-Competitive Section C.F. 31 to M.T.C. 4 – Quiet CRAG HALL – Quiet BROADGATE – Out-of-Bounds 182 964 – STOP at junction 180 964 – STOP at junction with A595
DAMAGE CONTROL	210 965	SW	–	–	Signed and completed DAMAGE FORMS MUST be handed in here
M.T.C. 4 FINISH	211 965	–	–	10	Standard Time 04.40 hrs at M.T.C. 4 [At the Reception Desk inside the Eccle Riggs Hotel] HAND IN TIME CARD 3

NOTES

F.D.M.C. Ltd "THE R.L. BROWN TROPHY RALLY '81" 19/20 September 81

Route Amendment

Saturday, 19th September 1981

* Due to WINSTER FORD being flooded, Non-Competitive Section C.F. 7 to C.S. 8 and Competitive Section 8 are modified as follows [Route Card page 2]

CONTROL	MAP REFERENCE	APPROACH	DEPART	TIME	COMMENTS
* Non-Competitive Section C.F. 7 to C.S. 8 – Out-of-Bounds 200 m. radius of 420 891½ – Strict Quiet WOODSIDE COTTAGE 426 895 – Strict Quiet BOWLAND BRIDGE
C.S. 8	413 896	SSE	NNW	6	
P.C. 'F'	407 892	NNE	SW		CARE ! – Steep downhill approach
C.F. 8	384 870	NE	SW	6	to Control C.F. 8
* Non-Competitive Section C.F. 8 to M.T.C. 2 (IN) – STOP at junction with A590
M.T.C.2 (IN)	375 856	NW	–	4	[Note – Time to M.T.C. 2 is now 4 minutes – not 8 minutes] HAND IN TIME CARD 1

* Maximum Lateness

* Has been modified as follows =

  1 From C.F. 6 to M.T.C. 2 (IN) (inclusive)   =   45 mins 59 secs
  2 From C.F. 12 to M.T.C. 3 (IN) (inclusive)   =   45 mins 59 secs
  3 At M.T.C. 4 (Finish)   "   "   "   =   45 mins 59 secs
  4 All other Sections remain at "   "   " =   30 mins 59 secs

THE ORGANISERS

	MAP REFERENCE	APPROACH	DEPART	TIME	COMMENTS
C.S. 7	399 837	S.	NE	4	Severe downhill hairpins 410 830 to 'X' 417 841
P.C. 'D'	406 834	S.	NE		
P.C. 'E'	415 870	SE	NNW		
C.F. 7	417 876½	W	NE	11	

CONTINUED PAGE ▷

JW8

J I M   C L A R K   M E M O R I A L   R A L L Y   –   1 9 7 4   R O U T E

NO SERVICING AREAS DENOTED BY:- 〔

	Location	App. From	References Start	Finish	Dep. To	Times 40mph	30mph	Remarks
Start	Duns	NE	782539		SW	1930	1930	
Via		N	772500					
SS1	Sisterpath I	NE	756483	736469	SE	1937 1-42	1939	
SS2	Charterhall I	N	755461	770½465	SE	1942 2-22	1946	
Via		NW	787440		SW			
Via		NE	702255		SSE			Quiet Ednam, Kelso
Via		N	695195		SE			
Via		NNE	679135		S			Quiet Oxnam
Fuel	Byrness	NW	771024					
	Service Area		780015					SP Camping Club of G.B.
M.C.1	Redesdale	W	820989½			2108	2108	SP Redesdale Camp
SS3	Bellshiel I	SE	819993	820042	SW	2108 8-47	2108	
SS4	Riverside I	S	819042	860115	SE	2121 9-49	2125	Maximum 30mph between Stage 4 Finish and Stage 5 Start TROUBLESOME FARMER!!!
SS5	Hindsike I	E	888063	940986	S	▬ 16-43	2151	
Via		N	943968		SW			Caution 942½980
SS6	Otterburn I	E	937954	856968	S	2204	2224	
CARD	COLLECTION		856960					HAND IN TIME CARD 1
Via			834850					
Via			834830					Quiet Bellingham
SS7	Pundershaw	NE	804807	729801		2234	2304	
SS8	Clintburn	NE	728802	773860		2244	2317	
SS9	Wellhaugh	E	660858	652897	▬	2303	2342	
Via			650901					
SS10	Bewshaugh	ENE	645905	623942½	SE	2314	2356	
								2 WAY RALLY TRAFFIC
SS11	Deadwater	S	623948	609976	S	2328	0015	
								2 WAY RALLY TRAFFIC
Fuel	Kielder		627934					
	Service Area		638913					

51ME RALLYE AUTOMOBILE MONTE-CARLO 1983

4ME ETAPE

ETAPE FINALE : " MONACO   -   MONACO " (100 VOITURES MAXIMUM)

COMMUNES	ROUTES	DISTANCES PART.	TOT.	HORAIRE APPROXIMATIF

JEUDI 27 JANVIER 1983

27me Secteur : "MONACO - ST PANCRACE " - 16 Km temps idéal : 0 H 40

COMMUNES	ROUTES	PART.	TOT.	HORAIRE APPROXIMATIF
MONACO	N 7			de 17 H 00 à 18 H 40
BIF N7/CD 37	CD 37	4,00		de 17 H 12 à 18 H 52
LA TURBIE	D 53	4,50	8,50	de 17 H 24 à 19 H 04
ST MARTIN DE PEILLE				
BIF D 53/ D 22	D 22	7,50	16,00	de 17 H 40 à 19 H 20

28me Secteur : "ST PANCRACE - MOULINET" - 65 Km -Temps idéal : 1 H 18

	COMMUNES	ROUTES	PART.	TOT.	HORAIRE APPROXIMATIF
	(Bif D 53 / D 22	D 22			de 17 H 42 à 19 H 22
22me	(COL DE LA MADONE				
E.C.	(ST AGNES	V 0			
	(COL DES BANQUETTES	V 7			
	(PEILLE	V 7	18,00	18,00	de 18 H 03 à 19 H 43
	Bif V 7 / D 53	D 53			
	LA GRAVE	D 53			
	Bif D 53 / D 21	D 21	6,00	24,00	de 18 H 11 à 19 H 51
	L'ESCARENE		7,00	31,00	de 18 H 19 à 19 H 59
	COL DE BRAUS	D 2204	10,00	41,00	de 18 H 31 à 20 H 11
	COL ST JEAN				
	SOSPEL	D 2566	12,00	53,00	de 18 H 45 à 20 H 25
	MOULINET	D 2566	12,00	65,00	de 19 H 00 à 20 H 40

Alpes
Maritimes.

29me Secteur : "MOULINET-(STMartin Vesubie) - ST SAUVEUR s/TINEE"

67,80 Km Temps idéal : 1 H 21

Nuit du Jeudi 27 au
Vendredi 28 Janvier

	COMMUNES	ROUTES	PART.	TOT.	HORAIRE APPROXIMATIF
	(MOULINET	D 2566			de 19 H 02 à 20 H 42
23me	(COL DE TURINI				
E.C.	(Bif D 2566 / D 70	D 70			
	(LA BOLLENE VESUBIE	D 70	22,40	22,40	de 19 H 29 à 21 H 09
	Bif D 70 / D 2565	D 2565	3,60	26,00	de 19 H 34 à 21 H 14
C.P.	ST MARTIN VESUBIE	D 2565	11,00	37,00	de 19 H 48 à 21 H 28
	COL ST MARTIN		9,00	46,00	de 19 H 58 à 21 H 38
	VALDEBLORE	D 2205	3,80	49,80	de 20 H 03 à 21 H 43
	ST SAUVEUR s/TINEE	D 30	18,00	67,80	de 20 H 23 à 22 H 03

Cartes Michelin N° 195 - 81

APPENDIX 5
Time cards

PASSAGEM Nº	ETAPA	H	M	S
	Chegada Arrivée Partida Depart			

CHC 3.2 - MARAMBAIA

	Tempo Time ⇄ Distância Distance			
8km		00	30	00
	Partida Depart Departure			

P. 3.1 - NOVOTEL - S. JOSÉ DOS CAMPOS

CONTROLES DE PASSAGEM
CONTROLES DE PASSAGE
PASSAGE CONTROLS

CONCORRENTE
CONCURRENT   Nº
COMPETITOR

Rallye Marlboro do Brasil
1981

S.JOSÉ DOS CAMPOS - MARAMBAIA - 00.30.00h

3	ETAPA ETAPE SECTION	1

Longines Electronic

CYTAX GARAGES RALLY

CAR No.

TIME CARD No. 4.

FAIL TIME – 12:39

8

Control No.	Code	Time	Penalty Points	Penalty Point
70				70
69				69
68				68
67				67
66				66
65				65
64				64
63				63
62	H	12-11		62
61	R	0 11		61
60	Rey	0.11		60
59	W	10		59
58	4	JAN		58
57	6	10,		57
MC 56	B	08	—	56 —
		TOTAL		

This Card to be handed in at T.C.70

APPENDIX 6
Pacenotes

Here are pace notes from 1982 Rothmans Manx International Rally used by Jimmy McRae (national champion)/Ian Grindrod (1), Ari Vatanen/Terry Harryman (2), Russell Brookes/Mike Broad (3) and Bertie Fisher/Austin Frazer (4).

It is interesting to note that Harryman and Frazer used a system of double dots to indicate an absolute bend — a bend that is taken flat out on every occasion, that Broad abbreviates the word tightens to 'titens' whereas Grindrod and Harryman uses the more common 'greater than' symbol.

Note also how Frazer uses many more items per page and Harryman keeps turning the pages more often, but his notes are much bigger. Note also the Irish spelling of the name of the stage in the case of Frazer!

Symbols used by the various co-drivers are as follows:

L = left	Q = quick
R = right	Lg = long
C = crest	S = slight
F = fast	o = flat
V = very	

18·27·36·43.

E̲A̲I̲R̲Y̲.   11·03Km.

S̲ᴛᴀʀᴛ @ ꜱɪᴅᴇ R̲ᴏᴀᴅ ᴏɴ L̲ᴇꜰᴛ.

L̈+R+L̈ 50

K̲ɪɴᴋꜱ̲ᴛᴏ̲ FL⊕ +

V̲F̲L̲ +/C + V̲F̲R̲ L̲g̲〉

+ FL 50

Eairy   18·27·36·43.

200 L̇ · L̇

V̲l̲g̲R̲̊ ̲t̲i̲t̲e̲n̲s̲+̲ ̲t̲i̲t̲e̲n̲s̲   KL̄ ~~E̶T̶ ̶t̶i̶t̶e̶n̶s̶~~ 50

R̊ 〉KL · R R̊

Q̲R̲ ̲t̲i̲t̲e̲n̲s̲ ̲t̲o̲ ̲j̲u̲m̲p̲ · QR · L̇ 100

L̇? L · T̲ᴜʀɴ̲ BR 100

L̇ 100

QR · L̇ E̲R̲ 50

lg L̇ R L̊ 100

ꜱ.ꜱ. 18:27:36:43   E̲I̲R̲E̲Y̲ (i)

S̲ᴛᴀʀᴛ

20 K̈ɪɴᴋꜱ + 50 L̈ + ᴋᴇᴇᴘ L̈ + Lg R̊/C + L̇

50 K̲ᴇ̲ᴇ̲ᴘ̲ R̈ ̲ɪ̲ɴ̲ᴛ̲ᴏ̲ L̇ + R̈ + R̈ (ᴀᴛ ʜꜱᴇ.)

+ Ṙ/ᴊᴜᴍᴘ + Ṙ + C̈ + L̈

100 L̈ + L̈ ɪ̲ɴ̲ᴛ̲ᴏ̲ ̲ᴛ̲ᴜ̲ʀ̲ɴ̲ F̲R̲. (ᴀᴛ ʜꜱᴇ)

100 L̈   70 Ṙ + Lg.L̇ + R̈ (ᴘᴀꜱᴛ ʜꜱᴇ.)

50 C̈ + L̈ + R̈ (ᴀᴛ ɢᴀᴛᴇ) + L̈

70 L̇   150 L̈/C + C̲ᴀ̲ᴜ̲ᴛ̲.⁵⁰ F̲R̲ + L̈

50 V̲F̲L̲ + Ṙ + L̈ + 50 R̈ + L̇/C (ꜱɪɢɴ)

100 C̈   70 L̈ (ᴀᴛ ᴘɪʟʟᴀʀ) 150 R̈

100 R̈ (ᴀᴛ ᴘᴏʟᴇꜱ) 50 L̈   50 L̈ (ᴘᴏʟᴇ)

50 Ṙ   50 R̈ (ᴀᴛ ᴘᴏꜱᴛ)   ⑩⓪

/26

Service schedule
for service crews

TEAM DATSUN EUROPE MONTECARLO RALLY 1980

NO	CREW	LOCATION	TIME CAR ZERO	SERVICE TIME	NEXT POINT DIST(KMS)	AV SPEED (KMS)	REMARKS
X1	S1,S2,M1	GAP DATSUN DEALER	SUN 20TH + 07.00	2 Hrs	93 Kms		Axle change and full service. M1 to OA with Rally car
OA	S1,S2,M1	Service Park at CHANTEMARLE before ice race	11.48	30 min (min)	S1 16 Kms / M1 25 Kms / S2 41 Kms		Tyre change for ice race
1A	S1	PRELLES Jct N94/D4 See P.3 roadbook	22.23	10 min	46 Kms	34	
1E	M1	L'ARGENTIERE LA BESSEE Jct D994E/D104 at BAR PMU/HOTEL DEL'INDUSTRIE Roadbook P.5	22.40		37 Kms	34	
2A	S2 (M1)	N94 between Kms 31.90 and Jct at Kms 35.64 P.6. Roadbook	23.09	5 min	57 Kms	36	
3A	S1,M1	On N94 between Jct with D40 (Kms 26.56 P.10) & D41 (Kms 34.46 P.11)	23.45	8 min	M1 - (max) 19 Kms / S1 - 80 Kms	29 / 34	
3E	M1	CHORGES - Jct N94/D3 (SP to Espinasses) P.14	MON 21ST 00.25		18 Kms	57	Follow Rally Car to 4A
4A	S2 (M1)	L'HOTEL on D900B at Jct with D3 P.14	00.44	10 min max	S2 - 181 / M1 - 72 Kms	44 / 53	

APPENDIX 8
Duties of rally officials

Stewards

They are not responsible with the organisation, having responsibility only to the RAC. They are to adjudicate in dispute or protests and can if necessary command a change or cancellation in the competition.

Clerk of the Course

Responsible for the general conduct of the rally, and will usually have planned the event from the start.

Secretary

Responsible for organisation of the event, though the entries are often dealt with by a separate Entries Secretary.

Scrutineers

Responsible for checking mechanical state of competing cars, both to ensure they comply with requirements of the event and the RAC but also that they are safe.

Marshals

Helpers working under the Clerk of the Course, responsible for detailed organisation, ranging from positioning cars at a control, manning junctions on a special stage to ensure nobody strays on to the stage through to the control marshals who time the cars and sign the road books.

Index